I0142084

FOREWORD BY REV. WERNER KNORR

RESTORATION
OF THE BACKSLIDDEN CHURCH

"The Earnest Desire of Our Lord Jesus
Christ for His Bride"

Ezekiel 37

Patrick Tamukong, Ph.D.

© *2017, All rights reserved.*

IEM PRESS is honored to present this title with the author. The views expressed or implied in this work are those of the author. IEM Press provides our imprint seal representing design excellence, creative content and high-quality production.

No part of this publication may be reproduced, stored in a retrieval system, or transmitted in any way by any means — electronic, mechanical, photocopy, recording, or otherwise — without the prior permission of the copyright holder, except as provided by USA copyright law.

Most scripture quotations are taken from the King James Version (KJV) of the Bible, a few others from the Living Bible (LB).

This book was first published in 2008 in Bamenda, Cameroon. This second edition has been much expanded.

ISBN-10: 1-947662-02-3
ISBN-13: 978-1-947662-02-5

Library of Congress Catalog Card Number: 2017913036

ENDORSEMENTS

Restoration is an incredibly poignant blueprint of how we can become the Church Jesus prayed for and thus awesomely delight the heart of God.

As one whose heart cries for a genuine return to the *old time Gospel,* I believe, Brother Patrick has a genuine burden from the Father, to take the Church back to the *ancient paths.*

Restoration represents God's mandate for His children. True revival cannot come to our Churches unless the distinctive characteristics outlined in this book control our hearts and minds. This book should be mandatory reading for Christians. Read it at least twice a year.

Rev. Dr. David Njemo; Former President,
Full Gospel Mission Cameroon.

This book, **Restoration,** is the heart cry of God for this generation. God wants to restore all things that the individual has lost before we can see the promised blessings and glory that God has in store for His people.

In this book, Brother Patrick brings together many insights and spiritual truths, both from the Old and New Testaments, which will vividly reveal to the Christian what he/she has lost, why it was lost, where it was lost, and how to recover and permanently keep it. I therefore recommend the book to all who want to enter into the promises of God for their lives. You will never regret or remain the same after reading it.

Rev. Solomon Kemamah; Littoral Area Supervisor,
Full Gospel Mission Cameroon

After reading through this book, I realized that the writer has a deep heart-cry on the situation of today's Church, which has been taken captive through worldliness.

God's displeasure (and judgment) at the Israelites at many different instances during the period of the Old Testament Patriarchs was often due to His people (the Israelis) copying the ways of the heathen, and becoming worldly. This is what took them to exile and captivity. If readers will read this book with opened spiritual eyes, they will see similar tears flowing from the writer's heart and eyes. And if they will join him to cry, the Lord will certainly hearken and restore His Church.

> *"But let man and beast be covered with sackcloth, and cry mightily unto God: yea, let them turn every one from his evil ways, and from the violence that is in their hands. Who can tell if God will turn and repent, and turn away from his fierce anger, that we perish not?"* **(Jonah 3:8-9).**

The Church of today needs books like this, which speak like a Patriarch of old, pointing out sin – God's enemy. This book is rich, and I believe that readers will come out with a word to tell.

Rev. Paul Ewome; Former Vice President,
Full Gospel Mission Cameroon.

At a time when the world is becoming "Churchy" and the Church worldly, this book has come to give the Church direction towards the essentials of true and practical Christianity.

Rev. T. H. Mbu-Arrey; South West I Area Supervisor,
Full gospel Mission Cameroon

Restoration of standards, blessings, focus, fellowship with God and unity in the Church are the greatest needs of the Church today. This book will be of much help to any minister or Christian who is crying for the fullness of God's Will in his/her ministry or personal life.

Ps. Gwanmesia Patrick; Pastor,
Faith Bible Church Douala-Cameroon.

This book is a practical solution to restoration crises that plaque the body of Christ in the developed and developing world. Brother Patrick in **Restoration** has explained scripturally how the Church was born out of genuine revival (after Pentecost) and experienced the Glory of God for a while. Yet, much has been lost and there is a great need for spiritual restoration. Patrick has done an excellent job of breaking down the subject of restoration into subtitles and has integrated God's Word into meaningful application of the principles of restoration that can help the body of Christ to better understand the way of spiritual restoration. Spiritual Restoration is a MUST and should be undertaken by all believers who have been trapped at the byway of the upward call of God.

Pius Mbu Oben, Ph.D.
Associate Professor and Coordinator of Fisheries &
Applied Animal Science Programs,
University of Buea, Cameroon.

This book is challenging! It will pull you out of your comfort zone and open your eyes to areas of your life where you have to fight hard in order to recover your full possessions in Christ!

Tchami Alphonse, M.D.
Full Gospel Mission Buea, Cameroon

To God be the glory and honor for putting into the heart of His son and servant this wonderful message of *"Restoration"*, which is the greatest need for the children of God in this generation; many of whom have abandoned the *ancient path.*

This book calls on the Church to go back to her roots and to be built again on the foundation of the Apostles and prophets, with Jesus Christ Himself as the chief corner stone **(Eph. 2:20-21).** Let everyone, called of God, read this book.

Elder Nchanji Cletus
Full Gospel Mission Bamenda, Cameroon

This book is a carrier of treasures that can change the life of a sincere Kingdom seeker forever. Considering the present state of the Church, what you now have in your hands is a "must read" as it presents the hope of Restoration for the fallen.

Marcellus F. Mbah, Ph.D.; Bournemouth University,
Bournemouth, United Kingdom

For the opportune length of time I have had to know Brother Patrick, it is not a surprise that a work of this magnitude would come out of him. The Biblical principles found in this book, if observed, shall certainly lead you to heaven in addition to ensuring a joyous Christian life here on earth. A careful summary can be found where he says, "Although things look so bad and hopeless, yet restoration is possible and must be".

Praise Wanchia; RCCG, Maryland, U.S.A.

At last, not all integrity has been lost. There are certainly thousands of prophets hidden by God who have not bowed down to the worldly way but can still condemn worldliness in strong terms. This book points to the **ancient path-**the path to full Restoration. I recommend it for all who are seeking true restoration from God.

Deacon Lankah Paul
Full Gospel Mission, Molyko Buea

DEDICATION

This book is dedicated to all faithful Saints who are burdened with the issue of **Restoration** or who have been groaning and yearning to see God rend the heavens and come down again to revive His Work.

CONTENTS

PART III

FOREWORD

Restoration and revival for the body of Christ are the issues that Brother Patrick Tamukong addresses in his book. The message is indeed very timely, as we see so much superficiality, loose living, carnality-even outright sin-in the lives of those who are named after Christ, including Church leaders.

The doctrines that Christians often hear nowadays, and live by, do not convey the true Gospel of Jesus, who said, "Ye shall know the truth, and the truth shall set you free", and who likewise said, "I am the truth". The Biblical Gospel focuses on Jesus; and right Christian living derives from an intimate relationship with Him, which will transform us more and more into His image.

Restoration of the Church of Jesus to its original state as it existed in the days of the Apostles, is what we need today. Oh, that God would grant us a fresh outpouring of His Spirit again: yes, such a mighty move that will deeply touch our innermost beings and convict of all secret and open sin. And may He anoint genuine men of God again, that they will proclaim the undiluted Gospel message with divine authority. The Word of God and the anointing of the Holy Spirit will bring about revival and restoration.

May also this present book, with a deep spiritual content, be mightily used by God to help bring about God's purposes for believers in these last days.

Rev. Werner Knorr; Germany
Pioneer Missionary, Full Gospel Mission Cameroon

PREFACE

This book was born when I had the opportunity to teach in our Church on **Restoration**. After preparing and delivering the teaching, my wife and I felt led by the Lord to organize the teaching into a book for His people.

When we read scriptures like **Ecclesiastes 3:14** *"... whatsoever God doeth, it shall be forever..."*; **1John 2:27** *"But the anointing which ye have received of Him abideth in you..."*; and **Romans 11:29** *"for the gifts and calling of God are without repentance"*, we may be tempted to think that when God does something to us or the Church, there can be no possibility of losing it. It is such thinking which has led some Christians into the erroneous doctrine of "Eternal Security" which asserts, in essence, that a believer in Christ cannot lose his/her salvation. In **Revelation 2:5**, however, God threatened to take away the candlestick (His Holy Spirit) from a compromising Church unless she repented. Likewise in **Revelation 3:5**, we read that those who fail to overcome will have their names eventually blotted out of the book of life. The Apostle Paul told the Galatians that they had begun in the Spirit but became carnal (**Galatians 3:3**). In **Hebrews 12:14-16**, we are warned to follow peace and holiness, watching carefully lest any of us in Christ falls away from God's grace or becomes profane like Esau who sold his birthright for a morsel of meat.

These, and the many other warnings given by our Lord Jesus Christ and His Apostles in the New Testament, clearly support the view that one's salvation can be lost, if not jealously guarded. Moreover, the blessings we receive in the Lord can be lost. Paul's exhortation to

Timothy to stir up the gift of the Spirit in his life (**2 Timothy 1:6**) suggests that the gift could lie dormant and die off. In other words, it could be lost if ignored.

Although God brought His people – the Israelis – out of Egypt determined to establish them in the Promised Land and bless them permanently, yet He was angry at them and overthrew most of them in the wilderness. Although the Church was born out of a genuine revival (after Pentecost) and experienced the glory of God for a while, yet by the fourth century AD, virtually all of this glory had been lost and the Church was silenced and plunged into the dark ages. Seasons of refreshing or revival have been experienced since then but these have not also been permanent. In the United States, for example, there have been good times when the Holy Spirit moved in unprecedented ways and great revivals were witnessed (such as the popular Azusa Street Revival), but these moves were never permanent.

Today's Church has been severely plagued by the devil and his hosts in many ways. She has fallen short of the glory of God and for most denominations or Church bodies, only a skeleton is left. The gold of the Christian Church (that is, her godliness) has become dim. Her precious sons initially comparable to fine gold have become mere earthen pitchers.

> *"How is the gold become dim! How is the most fine gold changed! The stones of the sanctuary are poured out in the top of every street. The precious sons of Zion, comparable to fine gold, how are they esteemed as earthen pitchers, the work of the hands of the potter!"* **(Lamentations 4:1-2).**

This was the shock of prophet Jeremiah regarding backslidden Israel. Israel lost her beauty; she lost the glory of God through compromise. By iniquity, Israel sold herself for nought, and became a captive covered with dust and ashes (**Isaiah 52:1-3**). **Gold** speaks of Divine nature. The more Israel sinned, the more her gold got dim and corrupted until it was reduced to earthen pitchers (*earth* speaks of the *flesh*). If Jeremiah came back to life today, he would cry even more for the end time Church which is in an adulterous marriage with the world system. Many tares have been sown while men slept. There is no longer a clear demarcation between the Church and the world. The two look the same in many ways. The Church is copying many things from the world whereas the world is copying little or nothing from the Church. In some parts of the world today, preachers are not allowed to even mention sin when proclaiming the Gospel. One hardly hears the prophets of today crying,

"Repent for the kingdom of God is at hand".

Preaching which points out sin and calls on sinners and compromising Christians to repent is rare nowadays. To many, pointing out sin is being critical or judgmental. Unfortunately, there can be no revival and restoration without deep repentance. Sinners and compromisers cannot repent without hearing a sound message which points out their sins vividly and urges them to repent.

This book partly describes what the Church has lost, where, and how to pursue it, with God's help, and experience full restoration. Although things look bad and even hopeless in some cases, yet restoration is possible and should be pursued. This is God's major pre-occupation now as we gradually draw to the end of the age. We are therefore sending out this book with many tears that God may use it to kindle a fire in every one who reads it. That we may each arise and seek the lost glory of the kingdom, paving the way for the return of our Lord Jesus Christ.

Patrick Tamukong, Ph.D.

ACKNOWLEDGEMENTS

I express profound gratitude to the following:

To Rev. W. Knorr for spiritual scrutiny. Out of his busy schedule, he was able to read through the first draft of this book line by line and to make necessary corrections.

To Rev. Dr. David Njemo, Rev. Solomon Kemamah, Rev. H. Mbu-Arrey, Rev. Paul Ewome, Ps. Gwanmesia Patrick, Dr. Oben Pius, and many others, whose counsel and impact on my life remain immeasurable.

To Full Gospel Church Molyko Buea, Cameroon where I was offered the opportunity to deliver a teaching on restoration which birthed this book.

To Elder Nchanji Cletus & Mr. Nokwang Isaac (of blessed memory) whom the Lord first used to plant the seed of the Gospel in my life and to **Rev. Fombang Daniel** who nurtured this seed in the early years of my Christian journey.

To Ms Katie Steffan who assisted with editing this second edition of the book.

To Gospel Press, Bamenda (Cameroon) for designing and printing the first edition of this book in 2008.

To my beloved wife, Dr. Delphine Tamukong (and kids), whose prayers and encouragement kept me pursuing this vision to full realization.

To the US Full Gospel Mission Fellowship in the United States, and US Full Gospel Mission in Grand Forks North Dakota in particular, where I have had the opportunity to serve the Lord and grow in His grace.

To IEM Press for publishing this book in the U.S.A.

To all others (friends, colleagues, etcetera) who have been a positive influence on my life.

May the Lord bless you all and credit your accounts in heaven.

INTRODUCTION

To restore is "to gain back that which was lost, taken or stolen". It also means "to clean and repair something old and dirty or damaged so that it looks the same as it did initially or even more glorious".

The bride of Jesus Christ (i.e., the Church) must be fully ready before her wedding day;

> *"let us be glad and rejoice, and give honour to Him: for the marriage of the Lamb is come, and His wife hath made herself ready"* **(Revelation 19:7)**.

This readiness will not happen arbitrarily or unconsciously. It must or has to be a deliberate cooperative work between the Lord Jesus Christ and His Bride, the Church. Before Jesus washed the feet of His disciples, He needed their cooperation. Peter resisted and would have been disowned, had he not yielded thereafter.

I have heard many people talk about the end time revival but I have scarcely heard them speak of what the Church has to do specifically for that to happen. There is a lopsided form of grace propagated especially in the United States nowadays. Grace that says "sit and do nothing because Christ did it all". Grace that says "it doesn't really matter how you live because Christ paid for your sins past, present, and future". The Ancient Serpent (Lucifer or Satan) who deceives the whole world is working ferociously and deceiving many. A biblical definition of grace can be found in **Titus 2:11-12**. This grace teaches us to shun all forms of ungodliness and worldly lusts, and to labor with God as the Apostle Paul did (**1 Corinthians 15:9-10**). God's grace is no license for laziness or careless living. It is also no guarantee that the treasures of the Kingdom given to us are ours forever irrespective of how we conduct our lives.

Many serious minded Christians admit the deplorable state of the Church in our time, but few are bothered about the way out of this spiritual decay. The Church has lost much of her glory. In **2 Chronicles 12:1-10**, we read of Shishak (a type of Satan and his cohorts), King of Egypt, who plundered Judah and carried away the treasures from God's Temple.

> [1]*And it came to pass, when Rehoboam had established the kingdom, and had strengthened himself, he forsook the law of the Lord, and all Israel with him.* [2]*And it came to pass, that in the fifth year of king Rehoboam Shishak king of Egypt came up against Jerusalem, because they had transgressed against the Lord,* [3]*With twelve hundred chariots, and threescore thousand horsemen: and the people were without number that came with him out of Egypt; the Lubims, the Sukkiims, and the Ethiopians.* [4]*And he took the fenced cities which pertained to Judah, and came to Jerusalem.* [5]*Then came Shemaiah the prophet to Rehoboam, and to the princes of Judah, that were gathered together to Jerusalem because of Shishak, and said unto them, Thus saith the Lord, Ye have forsaken me, and therefore have I also left you in the hand of Shishak.* [6]*Whereupon the princes of Israel and the king humbled themselves; and they said, The Lord is righteous.* [7]*And when the Lord saw that they humbled themselves, the word of the Lord came to Shemaiah, saying, They have humbled themselves; therefore I will not destroy them, but I will grant them some deliverance; and my wrath shall not be poured out upon*

Jerusalem by the hand of Shishak. [8] Nevertheless they shall be his servants; that they may know my service, and the service of the kingdoms of the countries. [9] So Shishak king of Egypt came up against Jerusalem, and took away the treasures of the house of the Lord, and the treasures of the king's house; he took all: he carried away also the shields of gold which Solomon had made. [10] Instead of which king Rehoboam made shields of brass, and committed them to the hands of the chief of the guard, that kept the entrance of the king's house (**2 Chronicles 12:1-10**).

Compare the above scenario with the account in **1 Samuel 30:1-20**. When the Amalekites plundered Ziklag and carried away all that David and his men had, David mobilized the people and pursued his enemies until he overtook them and recovered all that had been lost. For Rehoboam, the story was very different. Rather than pursue the enemy, Rehoboam made alternatives (of lower standard) for the treasures carried away from the Temple. He replaced the golden vessels carried away from the Temple with brass. This is very similar to what many Christians or Churches have done. Satan comes to kill, steal and destroy. Many Christians and Churches have been robbed by Satan. Many have a name (or fame) for being alive but are truly dead. Rather than arise, rend their hearts in deep repentance and pursue full recovery or restoration, they've devised alternatives of empty, impotent religious routines. Some Christians have gotten frustrated with their Pastors and Churches and have withdrawn from fellowship altogether. Others are going from one Church to another in search of what they lost.

Man has a tendency of seeking what he has lost or misplaced at the wrong places. When Mary and Joseph lost Jesus, they sought Him at the wrong places for three days (**Luke 2:42-51**). Going from Church to Church, or program to program may not necessarily lead you to the restoration you need. You need to arise, mobilize yourself as David did and wage war against the enemy. You need to learn the way of fervent tearful prayer. It is the singular way to true spiritual restoration. Sadly, few Christians know of this way in our time. Many talk the talk but can't walk the walk; many talk prayer but few truly pray; many sound spiritual but can't afford to stay for three days without food just to seek God's face in prayer. Yet, we need revival and restoration? Ours is a generation of religious clowns.

Again, restoration needs our cooperation with God. We can't stay aloof and yet, witness change in our lives and Churches. When Esther was to be prepared to stand before king Ahasuerus, she cooperated fully with Hegai and followed his instructions wholeheartedly.

> *"Now when the turn of Esther…was come to go in unto the king, she required nothing but what Hegai the king's chamberlain, the keeper of the women, appointed. And Esther obtained favour in the sight of all them that looked upon her"* (**Esther 2:15**).

The Lord Jesus Christ, by the Holy Spirit, is out to prepare His Church just as Hegai prepared Esther for Ahasuerus. The only difference is that Jesus is preparing the church to present to Himself. In **Ephesians 5:25-27**, we are told that Christ is purifying His Church to present to Himself as a chaste virgin without spot or wrinkle.

> *"Husbands, love your wives, even as Christ also loved the church, and gave Himself for it; that He might*

sanctify and cleanse it with the washing of water by the word, that He might present it to Himself a glorious church, not having spot, or wrinkle, or any such thing; but that it should be holy and without blemish" (**Ephesians 5:25-27**).

The word "spot" depicts any sin or dirt while the word "wrinkle" depicts any crookedness, lack of straightforwardness or integrity. "Without wrinkles" also implies "without old age which is characterized by lukewarmness, traditionalism and familiarity". Jesus is not coming to marry an old bride with grey hair and wrinkles. He is coming for a chaste virgin. The Apostle Paul said "*...though our outward man perish, yet the inward man is renewed day by day*" (**2 Corinthians 4:16**). Rather than grow spiritually old, get familiar with God and become nonchalant, we must continually be renewed, and fight off spiritual wrinkles as we await our Lord's return.

On the other hand, our Lord Jesus Christ is not coming for a very young maid without breasts. In **Song of Solomon 8:8-9**, we read of a young woman who would be unable to wed due to immaturity or the lack of breasts.

"We have a little sister, and she hath no breasts: what shall we do for our sister in the day when she shall be spoken for? If she be a wall, we will build upon her a palace of silver: and if she be a door, we will inclose her with boards of cedar" (**Song of Solomon 8:8-9**).

This little sister without breasts represents the unprepared, immature Christian or Church. Naturally, a girl without breasts will seldom attract a partner. Sadly, many within the Churches nowadays are like young breast-less women. Many are spiritually wretched, miserable, poor, blind and naked. Since they are blind, they do not know their condition at all or know so little about it that they are unconcerned. God expresses His worry over such a bride thus;

> "What shall we do for our sister in the day when she shall be spoken for?"

This is the worry of God the Father, Son and Holy Spirit. They are all thinking of what to do in order to make the Church ready for the "Marriage Feast of the Lamb". Your unpreparedness is a problem to the Godhead but you must cooperate to have this problem resolved. The Godhead continues,

> "If she be a wall, we will build upon her a palace of silver".

A few Christians nowadays are a *wall* that resists all manner of temptation. Such would strive against sin to the shedding of blood. They tolerate nothing foreign (from the flesh, the devil, or the world) to get into and pollute their lives. They are, as it were, a garden enclosed; a fountain sealed.

> "A garden inclosed is my sister, my spouse; a spring shut up, a fountain sealed" (**Song of Solomon 4:12**).

Such will be adorned; that is, "a palace of silver will be built on them". This means that they will be spiritually decorated for marriage, having on the white garment of righteousness. Yes, there are only a few "wall-like" Christians in today's Churches. Our Lord Jesus Christ mentioned that few find the narrow way.

The Godhead continues analysis of the situation of the Church as follows;

"...if she be a door, we will inclose her with boards of cedar". (**Song of Solomon 8:8-9**).

Many in the Church are *doors* with a readiness to yield to any temptation and compromise or lower divine standards at will. They love the easy path free from suffering. To such, the Godhead will do His best to enclose and protect from further defilement. Only after this can they be adorned for the marriage feast. If they rebel and remain as doors, they will be eventually disqualified.

"But From the Beginning, it was not so"

"He said unto them, Moses because of the hardness of your hearts suffered you to put away your wives: but from the beginning it was not so" (**Matthew 19:8**).

A lot of things have been introduced into God's Church which were not so from the beginning. Though the elders and fathers of the Church are fully aware of this and confess "this is not how we used to do" or "this is not how it was in our days", yet because of the hardness of the hearts of this generation, they are unable to speak against such strange practices. Consider, for example, the selling of God's grace, which is so common nowadays. It has become commonplace to pay money to receive healing or some other miracle from God. We now have to sow seeds for nearly every favor we want from God. Some preachers are now selling anointing oil, anointing water, special anointed stickers, aprons and handkerchiefs. Compare the greediness among the

clergy in our time to men like Elisha who refused gifts
for healing Naaman (**2 Kings 5**) or Peter who refused
money for the anointing (**Acts 8:18-23**). The difference
is very apparent.

Controversy has also crept into the Christian faith
on a good number of subjects. Such controversy as never
was since the origin of the Church. Sadly, few Christians
care about history. Church history shows that most of
the so-called controversial subjects within Christianity
today (e.g., the role of women in the Church) were not
controversial only some two centuries ago or less. Many
teachings and modern Bible translations which favor or
espouse wrong practices in the end time Church are also
very recently founded.

All of these result from a desire to make provision
for the flesh which leads men, who have been taken
captive by Satan or their own flesh, to tend to fight anything that takes them out of their comfort (fleshy) zones.
Many have become imitators of evil practices, who focus only on results, forgetting that "good results" do
not make "evil practices" right. The world's definition
of success is at variance with God's definition. What is
highly esteemed among men is abomination with God
(**Luke 16:15**). Do not focus on the outward appearance.

Modern Christians, who have adopted worldly ways
of living, tend to criticize the olden day believers, and
view such as primitive and ignorant in multiple ways.
Many have dared to challenge teachings of Church fathers like the Apostle Paul. Such boldness is the same
kind which was in Lucifer when he arose in heaven to
challenge God and exalt his own throne. Needless to
state that despite the increase in knowledge in our time,
we are yet to witness a fraction of the glory and power
which manifested in the early Church, among the so-
called "primitive" or "ignorant" Christians. We rather

have more of soulish power in our time in lieu of true Holy Ghost anointing. We have more of psychologists and entertainers at our pulpits as opposed to ministers of true life. One would find a man preaching vigorously and perspiring from head to feet Sunday after Sunday. Yet, his congregation is filled with sensuality, immorality and all else that characterizes the flesh. So what kind of power is at work in such a preacher? Certainly not the power of the Holy Ghost. Jesus said when the Holy Spirit comes, He convicts of sin. The hallmark of a genuine anointing is that it convicts of sin and ushers holiness. So much of what we have out there nowadays is "soulish power".

The above analyses are meant to show that restoration is a genuine need for the Church today. We need restoration in our individual lives and Churches. Having begun in the Spirit, many Churches are being perfected in the flesh. The flesh is like cancer and when a little space is provided, it grows rapidly and multiplies like weed on a farm, overshadowing the Spirit. We are told to walk in the Spirit and not gratify the desires of the flesh (**Galatians 5:16**). We must not leave room for the flesh. Be careful with what you permit today because you may not deal with or confront it easily tomorrow.

Finally, though we have lost many things and fallen short of the glory of God, full restoration is possible. This is the reason for this book. Let us now move on to discuss what has been lost.

PART I

WHAT THE CHURCH HAS LOST

Without knowledge of what is lost, the tendency is to pursue anything or perhaps settle in mediocrity, satisfied with mercy drops. Ignorance could, otherwise, lead one to accept something less than full restoration. God took time to describe the inheritance He gave to Abraham. He did the same to Isaac and then to Jacob. To Jacob's children (the Israelis), God gave details of the dimensions of the land (see **Numbers 34:6, 11-12, Exodus 23:31, Deuteronomy 11:24**). This was very important. God never leaves anyone in oblivion. If we walk closely with Him, He will clarify His Will to each of us. **Amos 3:7** says *"Surely the Lord GOD will do nothing, but he revealeth his secret unto his servants the prophets"*. If you are confused in your life, seek the Lord. Jesus said those who walk in the light do not stumble. He exhorted His disciples to walk while they had the light with them (**John 12:35-36**). Jesus Himself is that Light who lights every man born into the world. If we walk with Him, He will clarify the dimensions of our inheritance or ministry.

Israel needed to know the dimensions of what God had given them. Due to their rebellion against God, they were judged and scattered overseas, away from their

God-given inheritance. Therefore their enemies occu-
pied the land. Although the Jewish people returned and
founded the State of Israel in modern times, it has been
difficult to completely root out their enemies who now
view them as "Occupiers" in their own land. Despite
the resistance Israel faces in modern times, the Jewish
people have not forgotten the biblical dimensions of the
land accorded to them by the Lord.

How about you? Do you understand the hope of
your calling in Christ? Have the things freely given to
you as a child of God been revealed to you by the Holy
Spirit (**1 Corinthians 2:9-12**)? Are you aware of what
you've lost or forfeited since coming to the Lord? Unless
we address very personal questions, and unless we fully
understand our loss, we cannot seek restoration. Some
Christians have lost their ability to pray, fast, evangelize
and give as before. Others have grown cold spiritually,
compromised standards, and/or lost spiritual gifts. It is
not God's wish that we lose the things we receive from
Him. The Apostle John warned *"Look to yourselves, that
we lose not those things which we have wrought, but that
we receive a full reward"* **2 John 1:8**. We must guard the
things we receive from the Lord. We must guard our
salvation and gifting. If you received a gift of prophecy
from God, heaven expects you to guard that gift jealously, trade with it, bring profit into the Kingdom of God
through it, and give an account about it on the last day.
In the Parable of the Talents, the servant who buried his
talent was judged. What then shall happen to those servants who lose their talents? We can only imagine.

Sadly, the Church (and by Church, I'm referring to
you and me) has not preserved the things the Holy Spirit wrought within her. We've gone far into compromise
and worldliness that returning seems difficult. Many
no longer know their way back to God. The "Ancient

Path" spoken of in **Jeremiah 6:16** has been completely blurred or obscured and unpopular (well, it always has been unpopular through the ages; only few are usually on the narrow way in every generation). Failure to understand what we've lost makes us settle for less. You see, because Peter was unaware of Pentecost and the glory awaiting him, he desired to remain at the mount of transfiguration (**Matthew 17:4**); while Nathanael was contented just seeing Jesus for the first time, not knowing the greater things that were ahead (**John 1:49-51**). Likewise, the tribes of Reuben and Gad were satisfied with the plains of Jazer and Gilead, ignorant of what the Promised Land had for them. They were quick to settle for what was less than God's initial intention for them (**Numbers 32:1-5**). Needless to mention that these tribes were the first of the Israeli tribes to go into captivity. It is dangerous to end on the way or settle for what is less than God's total intention for your life. The next three chapters will unfold to us what the Church (that is, you and me) has lost.

CHAPTER ONE

THE WORK OF THE PALMERWORM, LOCUST, CANKERWORM, AND CATERPILLAR.

The activities of these organisms depict things in the Church that have resulted in lack of intimacy with God (characterized by the absence of quality time in prayer, no Bible meditation, no holiness and integrity), and disunity among the brethren.

Although God is jealous for His people (His Church) and desires to bless them permanently, yet the foolishness and rebellion of God's people has always compelled Him to surrender His heritage to reproach. God cannot stand the presence of sin. His love is quite strong but often overcome by sin. King David knew this very well and declared,

> *"For thou art not a God that hath pleasure in wickedness: neither shall evil dwell with thee. The foolish shall not stand in thy sight: thou hatest all workers of iniquity. Thou shalt destroy them that speak leasing: the Lord will abhor the bloody and deceitful man"* (**Psalms 5:4-6**).

There are many heretical preachers nowadays whose preaching and teachings espouse the notion that God loves us so much that He will not allow us to perish, for Jesus has already paid the full price for our sins; past, present and future. God therefore takes responsibility for all our sins. If it were so, the Bible would not warn in **Hebrews 10:26** that if we sin willfully, no sacrifice remains for sin. **Romans. 11:21** also reads,

"For if God spared not the natural branches, take heed lest He also spare not thee".

God is angry at the wicked everyday (**Psalms 7:11**). His wrath is revealed from heaven against all ungodliness and unrighteousness of men (**Rom. 1:18**). This is what forces Him to remove our defense and to strengthen our enemies against us. Though God may test the righteous as He did with Job, yet most of the chastisement and defeats we suffer are a consequence of our rebellion against God. The wise Psalmist said,

"Before I was afflicted, I went astray ..." (**Psalms 119:67**).

Let us now turn to the Book of **Joel** to see the devastating work of the enemy on God's Church and our individual lives. The Lord, in seeking to put the situation in a way that these Israelites in their own time could easily understand, likened it to the effect of insects on plants. This was because the Israelites were mostly farmers and grazers. Note that virtually everything in the Bible has a spiritual connotation. Thus, God was not just talking here about the work of palmerworms, locusts, etcetera on vines and crops but more about spiritual decay and the work of Satan and his cohorts on the Church. For *"The thief cometh not, but for to steal, and to kill, and to **destroy**..."* (**John 10:10a**). Therefore whenever you see destruction (of what is good) in the Bible, you can safely link that with the works of Satan. God also uses Satan and his elements to judge His people. For example, in judging Saul, the first king of Israel, God sent an evil spirit upon him to torment him (**1 Samuel 19:9**). Let's now read from the book of Joel.

> *"Hear this, **ye old men**, …Hath this been in your days …? … That which the palmerworm hath left hath the locust eaten; and that which the locust hath left hath the cankerworm eaten; and that which the cankerworm hath left hath the caterpillar eaten"* (**Joel 1:2-4**).

The cry begins with "Hear this, ye **old men**". You see, it is the old men (who had had old good days) who can really fully understand what has been lost and the extent of damage. They are the ones who can raise a mighty cry to the Lord, mindful of the height from which we are fallen. As for the young (who may not have witnessed days of glory), these may easily settle for mercy drops, and can only cry if they receive a revelation regarding what they are missing. Given that the Prophet Joel asked, *"hath this been in your days?"* signifies that the old days had been good and these old men had witnessed those days. The "old men" in every Church, the leaders, ought to take the lead in the battle for restoration. As God urged the Priests in the book of Joel to call for fasting and prayers, so Church leaders or the "old men" of our time ought to sound the trumpet in Zion and call the Church to deep repentance. What do the insects in **Joel 1** represent? Let's see their evil work on plants and the corresponding spiritual implications.

THE PALMERWORMS

Palmerworms destroy fruits and eat the roots of plants. Roots support and absorb water and mineral salts from the soil for the plant. Thus, when the palmerworms finish their mission, the affected plant is left fruitless as the fruit falls off (and eventually the plant too).

Therefore palmerworms represent evil spirits or those devices of Satan whose ultimate intent is to render our lives and the Church fruitless and powerless; to cut us off from our source of supply so that we lack stamina and can easily be blown off. The Apostle Paul mentioned that Christ is the foundation on which every life is built spiritually (**1 Corinthians 3:11-13**). Likewise **Colossians 2:7** exhorts us to be deeply rooted in Christ. Therefore Christ is the foundation and ground for our growth; He is the anchor for our souls and the ground of our Christian faith. Palmerworms undermine this and labor to detach the Christian from this foundation. When one looks at the contemporary Church, the work of the palmerworms is quite evident. Many professing Christians are very carnal or superficial. Many are easily tossed by any wind of doctrine. I read a disgusting article online recently about a pastor who fed his congregants with live serpents "in the name of the Lord"! What a shame. It is unimaginable that those simple minded Christians consume those snakes. There are many abominable practices going on in Churches nowadays which lend credence to the superficiality or carnality in the Christian faith. This carnality shows that palmerworms have been eating our roots. The average Christian today cannot afford a regular daily hour of prayer and Bible meditation, not to mention blocking out time to go on a personal spiritual retreat. Palmerworms ensure that we get too busy for anything that lead to a deepening of our faith in Christ. The result is spiritual dryness and the absence of spiritual power.

Jesus said,

> *"I am the vine, ye are the branches...without me, ye can do nothing"* (**John 15:5**).

And again,

> *"As the living Father hath sent me, and I live by the Father: so he that eateth me, even he shall live by me"* (**John 6:57**).

Paul said,

> *"...I live by the faith of the Son of God..."* (**Galatians 2:20**).

As mentioned previously, Jesus Christ is like soil and we are like plants which must remain attached to the soil to daily tap nutrients from Him in order to stay alive spiritually. Palmerworms labor to break this intimacy. Palmerworms could manifest through your job, business, spouse, children, ministry and etcetera. Yes, ministry could become a palmerworm if it takes the place of our having to seek God for intimacy and a deepening of our roots in Him. In **Song of Solomon 1:6** we read,

> *"Look not upon me, because I am black, because the sun hath looked upon me: my mother's children were angry with me; they made me the keeper of the vineyards; but mine own vineyard have I not kept"*

A keeper of vineyards is a person in ministry, taking care of other lives. In the above Scripture, a minister laments on failure to keep his own personal life while busy with ministry. The ministry had become a palmerworm. I know a renowned gospel minister whose marriage fell apart. This man later testified that his marriage collapsed because he got so absorbed with ministry and ignored his wife. So yes, a good thing can become a palmerworm.

Examine yourself. Do you still stand sure or have your roots been affected? Are you still living in deep fellowship with the Holy Spirit or are you now being perfected in the flesh? Are you still holding tenaciously to the Gospel of your salvation (**2 Thessalonians 2:15**) or are you gradually replacing that with New Age theology? Sincere answers to these (and other similar) questions will reveal whether palmerworms are at work in your life or not.

THE LOCUSTS

These are short horned grasshoppers which eat up every green thing on their path so to speak. They destroy plant leaves. The leaves of a plant are the location where food is manufactured for the plant. What does this mean spiritually? The Word of God is the only food for our spiritual lives. Therefore, locusts are demons or anything assigned to attack the Word of God in our lives and the Church at large.

The Parable of the Sower (**Mark 4:1-8**) clearly illustrates what locusts could possibly represent spiritually. In this parable, we see that Satan attacks God's Word in our lives in various ways. There are the fowls of the air (flying demons) who devour the Word in the lives of some Christians as soon as they hear it; other evil elements are in charge of hardening hearts and making them stony and repulsive to the growth of the Word; while other Satanic elements are assigned to stir up worldly cares, anxieties and the desire for riches in order to render the Word of none effect in some lives. The end result is barrenness or emptiness and the prevalence of false doctrine with many being swept away as is the case today. A barren life is a life void of the Word of God and the Holy Spirit. It will not be an exaggeration to say that the Church (that is, the global Church) has lost her freshness (her ability to function as the "salt of the earth" or "light of the world") in many ways.

Leaves equally speak of hope and fruitfulness. That is why when Jesus saw a fig tree with leaves, he went to it expecting to find fruits **(Mark 11:13).** A plant without leaves obviously lacks food and consequently, fruits.

The locusts waging war against the End Time Church are far from ordinary. Indeed, they are similar to those which shall ascend out of the bottomless pit in the tribulation era to wreak havoc on the earth.

> *"And the shapes of the locusts were like unto horses prepared unto battle; and on their heads were as it were crowns like gold, and their faces were as the faces of men. And they had hair as the hair of women, and their teeth were as the teeth of lions. And they had breastplates, as it were breastplates of iron; and the sound of their wings was as the sound of chariots of many horses running to battle. And they had tails like unto scorpions, and there were stings in their tails: and their power was to hurt men…"* **(Revelation 9:7-11).**

We must each examine ourselves again to see the quality of God's Word in our lives. I met a lady who claimed to be a child of God but was under a terrible demonic oppression. Her pastor had taught her to carry a bottle of olive oil around which she could sprinkle her body and house with each time she sensed the presence of demons. She had been doing this for a long time but was never free. Here is an example of false teachings and such examples abound nowadays. Throughout the Bible, we never find olive oil being used for scaring away demons. Jesus cast out demons with the Word of God (**Matthew 8:16**) or by the Finger of God; that is, the Holy Spirit (**Luke 11:20**). Today, doctrines which undermine the power of the Scriptures and the Holy Spirit and emphasize physicals such as olive oil, special anointing water, special rings and etcetera are many. Such replacements of truth with heresy testify to the work of locusts on the Church and our individual lives. Locusts labor to dilute the truth of God's Word and to replace this truth with a lie. There are many preachers nowadays whom one could sit and listen to for an hour and not be able to state any substantial biblical truth gained from the message. Such preachers have been sifted or emptied by locusts. Have you ever seen a tree eaten by locusts? Such trees would usually look pale and leave-less. Such is the condition of some lives in today's Church. May the Lord help us to have salt in ourselves; that the Word of Christ may dwell in us richly in all wisdom (**Colossians 3:16**). May we not be victims of end time locusts.

THE CANKERWORMS

These worms burrow tunnels into the branches and trunks of trees, causing them to fall over. How does this relate to us spiritually? You know, a standing tree speaks of a standing person or Church, and this speaks of righteousness or holiness and integrity. In **Isaiah 61:3** we read,

"...that they might be called trees of righteousness,
the planting of the LORD, *that he might be glorified".*

Here, the Lord referred to His people as "trees of
righteousness" after they would have been restored.
Other Scriptures such as **Psalms 1:3**, **Psalms 52:8** and
Psalms 92:12 testify of faithful Christians as trees by the
riverside, olive or palm trees in God's house. Therefore
the attack of insects on plants as given in the "parable"
in **Joel 1** relates with our lives. Especially, the mission of
cankerworms is to destroy holiness and integrity so that
instead of standing straight or upright in the Lord, we
are bent or fallen.

In the End Time Church, integrity is a scarce virtue. Since difficult times have come upon our generation, many have learned to tell lies and cheat, including
Church folks. The number of gospel ministers with fake
credentials is on the rise. It is not uncommon nowadays
to pay money online and be awarded a doctorate in ministry. Lying wonders are also more common in today's
Church. I have heard stories of Christians obtaining
"blessings" through lying and in turn, giving testimonies about these in their Churches. A brother in the Lord
told me of one of such cases recently. He mentioned that
the lady involved in lying quoted Abraham who lied
in Egypt but was still blessed of the Lord. Beloved, do
not join the multitudes to commit evil. When King Saul
reserved the best of the sheep from the Amalekites and
claimed he intended to offer them to the Lord as a sacrifice, he was considered by God as a rebellious servant
and hence, disqualified from being King. As far as God
is concerned, obedience is better than sacrifice.

How about marriages breaking apart? Many Christians are liars in the sense that they easily break marriage vows through divorce. Oh, that ugly word which

has become so common in today's Church. Divorce was once a taboo among God's people but not so anymore. As the Church has gotten increasingly worldly and her members increasingly selfish, divorce rates have likewise accentuated. Although there are always many good reasons divorcees give to justify their actions, divorce is a breach of covenant and shows lack of personal integrity with regards to the confessions (marriage vows) the victims had made during their marriage. If you are reading this book and are still single, I would advise you not to repeat statements from your pastor (or officiating minister) without careful thought on your wedding day. Do not utter words on your wedding day which you may not honor throughout your life. It is best not to utter words presumptuously than to be a liar and covenant breaker.

How about greedy pastors who are making hundreds of thousands of dollars from rather poor congregants? When one looks at how such monies are raised, it can be saddening. Quite often, a plea is made to raise funds for some form of philanthropic activity. Otherwise, simple minded Christians are lured to sow financial seeds into the gospel minister in order to gain favors from God. The monies collected this way are used to build mansions and buy private jets for such gospel ministers. How can we possibly explain how a gospel minister collects tithes and offerings from poor Church members, opens a college with that money, and the same poor congregants are unable to send their children to the said college because they cannot afford tuition and other costs? This is not fiction, it actually happened somewhere. These unscrupulous practices testify to the work of the cankerworms on the End Time Church.

Pause here and examine your own life personally. How is your walk with the Lord? Do you feel cankerworms have been encroaching on you? Have you start-ed compromising? Are there things you knew to be sinful and rejected vehemently when you first believed, but today you are gradually tolerating? Have you start-ed telling lies? Are you drifting from your integrity or are you still standing firm like Job? Job said,

> "...till I die I will not remove my integrity from me" **(Job 27:5b).**

Trustworthiness is no longer an attribute of many lives in God's Church. Loss of personal integrity is an indication that cankerworms are at work in a man's life.

THE CATERPILLARS

These are worm-like larvae of moths and butterflies which also feed on plant leaves, but whose primary function is to help decompose tree trunks and roots. This is the final stage of decay in the Church; that is, **decomposition** or **disintegration.** This speaks of de-struction of the unity of the Body of Christ for which He prayed earnestly before His departure from the earth. Jesus prayed passionately for the Church to be one. He prayed for this oneness to be as intimate as that existing within the Holy Trinity. Not only would this serve as a strong witness to the world, such oneness is the basis for symmetric spiritual growth wherein each member of the Body is well nourished and established. The Bible says,

> "From whom the whole body fitly joined to-gether and compacted by that which every joint supplieth, according to the effectual working

in the measure of every part, maketh increase
of the body unto the edifying of itself in love"
(**Ephesians 4:16**).

This is what the Church ought to be; fully compact-
ed, with each joint supplying to the body according to its
own measure of grace. Unfortunately, caterpillars have
attacked the Church, causing the present noticeable numerous factions and disunity. As noted above, these
caterpillars represent spiritual forces or anything else
charged with destroying unity and fellowship among
brethren. Any individual whose mission at a Church is
to slander Church members, gossip and sow discord is
a caterpillar. Such a person is not serving the Lord; he or
she is not helping Jesus gather but is scattering abroad.
There are six things the Lord hates and the seventh is an
abomination, which is,

"...he that soweth discord among brethren" (**Proverbs**
6:19).

We must take heed to ourselves such that at no time
should we be used against God's work as caterpillars.
It's easy to slip into this snare. Some personal assessment questions are in order here. How are you using
your mouth? How do you relate with other believers in
Christ? Are you with Jesus or you are against Him? Are
you helping Him to gather or you are scattering abroad?
Honest responses to these questions will help you see if
caterpillars have affected your life or ministry. Indeed,
caterpillars have eaten into and decomposed many families, marriages, Churches, denominations and etcetera.
Arise and wage war against these spiritual bulldozers of
the evil one. Unity must return to your marriage, family
and God's Church in this restoration era.

CHAPTER TWO

THE LOSS OF THE WALLS AND GATES OF THE CHURCH

This speaks of the loss of salvation or Divine protection, sound ministration of the Word, zeal for evangelism, morals/ethics, livelines, dominion, God's effective presence, purity and satisfaction.

The Church has **walls** and **gates** just as was the case with the city of Jerusalem.

OUR WALLS

Every child of God has a spiritual wall around him or her and the Church at large has a spiritual wall around her. About Job, Satan testified

> *"Hast not thou made a hedge about him, and about his house, and about all that he hath on every side?..."* **(Job 1:10)**.

Satan prowls around like a roaring lion, always in search of careless victims to devour. He must have attempted hurting Job multiple times and must have failed each time due to the protective wall God had established around Job and all he owned. Satan could describe this wall in detail. He knew the wall was on every side because he had probably attempted penetrating Job on every side. He also knew the wall was about everything belonging to Job because he had possibly attempted destroying Job's possessions and children, having failed to hurt him directly. Dear friend, we have a real enemy who seeks our destruction daily. This enemy is not your "bad" spouse, or child, or neighbor, or colleague, or boss. This enemy is invisible. The United States spends billions of dollars annually on counter-terrorism. But the real enemy is always invisible. This is why it has been difficult to annihilate terrorism. It's like fighting a deadly cancerous tumor. The cells just keep multiplying. The enemy is invisible and remote-controls or uses those who pledge allegiance to him. This is why after successfully killing the "most wanted terrorist", quite often, much more wicked ones arise.

Heaven warned us as follows

"...Woe to the inhabiters of the earth and of the sea! for the devil is come down unto you, having great wrath, because he knoweth that he hath but a short time" (**Revelation 12:12**).

Satan has come to us here on earth, he came for you and me. We are His target; he is filed with great wrath due to the shortness of his time. But the Lord has not left us at the mercy of Satan. We are hidden (from Satan) with Christ in God (**Colossians 3:3**). Howbeit, if we break the hedge of protection through sin or compromise, we would become vulnerable to satanic attacks and possible destruction (**Ecclesiastes 10:8**). But until then, God Himself promises to be a wall about us.

"For I, saith the Lord, will be unto her a wall of fire round about, and will be the glory in the midst of her" (**Zechariah 2:5**).

"As the mountains are round about Jerusalem, so the Lord is round about His people from henceforth even for ever" (**Psalms 125:2**).

These walls are meant for protection and salvation.

" ...thou shalt call thy walls Salvation, and thy gates Praise" (**Isaiah 60:18**).

The word **salvation** is derived from the Greek word "**sétèria**" which means "deliverance", "bringing safely through", or "keeping from harm". Thus, the Lord jealously guards His people who fear Him, and keeps them safe from the Satan and his cohorts.

The question of whether a Christian can be oppressed, afflicted, or possessed by demons is one of debate among Bible Scholars. Some Christians believe this is possible while others believe once a person is saved, Satan cannot maintain his hold on that individual. I hold that when we come to Christ, the grip of sin and the Devil is broken over us and a hedge of salvation is built around our lives. In other words, we are hidden with Christ in God according to **Colossians 3:3**. If, however, the believer in Christ does not walk faithfully with the Lord, the hedge can be broken, exposing him/her to possible demonic oppression, affliction and even possession.

Today, it is not uncommon to find Church members oppressed by Satan. Some Churches have regular deliverance services or special meetings for breaking curses. The same Church members respond to Altar calls for such prayers day in day out and no permanent deliverance is experienced. These empty routines are caused by two things: either ignorance on the part of the oppressed Christian (Christ said we shall know the truth which would make us free), or sin and compromise which have broken the hedge around that Christian. Once this hedge is broken, deliverance prayers are meaningless or even dangerous because the driven demons would return with seven more vicious demons to inhabit those lives.

The End Time Church is an army which has lost battles on multiple fronts. On the European continent, for example, many former Church buildings are now Islamic Mosques. Most existing Churches are spiritually dead and filled largely with the aging population. In my home town here in the U.S.A., Muslims recently bought over a Church building and transformed it into a Mosque.

Worldliness or carnality in the End Time Church has resulted in broken walls and consequently, many successful attacks from the Kingdom of Darkness. Many Christians have been bitten (by the Ancient Serpent) in their marriages, jobs, businesses, health, ministries, etcetera; all because of broken walls. There are cries and sighs in the Church caused by the enemy. How did he come in? While men slept (**Matthew 13:25**).

Sleep is next to death and speaks of lukewarmness, laziness, indifference and sin. Our walls have been broken down as a result of sin; for God promised to take away our hedge if we do not keep the terms of the covenant; that is, to walk in absolute obedience to Him. The ever increasing divorce rates, fornication, cohabitation, unwanted pregnancies especially among Christian teens, sensual dressing, etcetera common in the Church nowadays are a testament to the attacks of the Ancient Serpent on the Daughter of Zion. Oh Church

"Awake, awake; put on thy strength, O Zion; put on thy beautiful garments, O Jerusalem, the holy city: for henceforth there shall no more come into thee the

uncircumcised and the unclean. Shake thyself from the dust; arise, and sit down, O Jerusalem: loose thyself from the bands of thy neck, O captive daughter of Zion. For thus saith the Lord, Ye have sold yourselves for nought; and ye shall be redeemed without money" (**Isaiah 52:1-3**).

OUR GATES

The Church as well as our personal lives equally has **gates** or **entry points**. A look at the walls and gates of Jerusalem, the city of God, will help us at this point in understanding the gates of the Church; many of which are closed, partly opened, or demolished by the enemy. You know Jerusalem also speaks of the Church.

Nehemiah championed the reconstruction of the walls and gates of Jerusalem in the time of the restoration of Israel. Due to sin and compromise in Israel, the Lord had strengthened King Nebuchadnezzar of Babylon who conquered the Jewish people, destroyed Jerusalem's wall and gates, and took many Jews prisoner. Some seventy years after Babylonian captivity, Nehemiah, Ezra and other Jews returned to rebuild the walls of Jerusalem and to seek spiritual and physical restoration.

The walls of Jerusalem had **ten** significant gates, which are an allegory of the ministries or graces of the Church. As we examine these gates, Satan's attack on the Church will become more and more vivid. Turn with me to **Nehemiah chapter Three** and let's examine these gates.

THE SHEEP GATE

*"Then Eliashib the high priest rose up with his brethren the priests, and they built the **sheep gate**; they*

sanctified it, and set up the doors of it; even unto the tower of Meah they sanctified it, unto the tower of Hananeel" **(Neh. 3:1).**

The **sheep gate** symbolizes the ministry of the pastors, the bishops or elders, etcetera, who look after the sheep or God's flock. In **John 21:15-17**, Jesus told Peter thrice to feed His sheep. Also, in **Jeremiah 3:15**, God promised to give to the Church pastors according to His heart who will feed her with knowledge and understanding. Nevertheless, today this gate has suffered severe attacks.

There are many self-made ministers who are enemies of the cross of Christ; whose god is their belly; who feed themselves instead of the sheep; and who are out to propagate themselves instead of the Gospel of our Lord Jesus Christ. They have not resolved like Paul to know nothing else except Christ crucified. The Lord didn't send them, yet they went in His name (**Jeremiah 23:21**). In today's Church, there are many Gospel ministers who lack a solid foundation in God's Word and who teach half-truths or outright heresy. Many are in ministry just for the money or benefits they can get. Ministry has become just another job like the secular ones. It is hard to find selfless servant leaders who love nothing but God and hate nothing but sin.

Time will fail me narrating some of the things I have witnessed. I watch one minister boast on TV who said he was a great man and that no one could bring him down. Yes, many are boastful nowadays, and many are decorated with titles they cannot truly defend. Many churches are sick today because the entire head is sick; that is, the leadership (**Isaiah 1:5-6**). Yes, as one man put it, "there are no dead Churches, there are only dead pulpits". If the foundation is destroyed, what can the righteous do? **(Psalms 11:3).**

In a time of restoration, Jesus Christ, the Great Shepherd of the sheep, Himself arises to purge His Church from fake leaders and to feed His flock

"I will feed my flock, and I will cause them to lie down, saith the Lord God. Therefore will I save my flock, and they shall no more be a prey; and I will judge between cattle and cattle. And I will set up one shepherd over them, and he shall feed them, even my servant David; he shall feed them, and he shall be their shepherd" **(Ezekiel 34:15 & 22-23).**

David in the above Scripture is a type of Christ. Christ is the Good Shepherd who lays down His life for His flock. He said *"my sheep hear my voice and they follow me..."*. Correct ministry is Christ doing His work (feeding His flock), howbeit with the use of human vessels. None of us can work for God; none of us can do His work acceptably. Without Him, we can do nothing, and nothing means nothing. Actually, without Jesus, we can do some "good" things for God, but before Him, it would amount to nothing. This is why the Apostle Paul said

"But we have this treasure in earthen vessels, that the excellency of the power may be of God, and not of us" **(2 Corinthians 4:7).**

The sheep gate of the Church needs to be restored so that the genuine Word of God can again flow from our pulpits through the Holy Spirit. Healed pulpits will lead to healed pews. This is the only way we can ensure restoration and revival in our Churches. It is very important that this gate is named first in **Nehemiah 3**. This is not accidental; it speaks to the critical importance of this gate. It should be noted that this gate was repaired by the High Priest and his brethren. To heal our pulpits, we must return to Christ, our faithful High Priest in the order of Melchizedek.

THE FISH GATE

*"But the **fish gate** did the sons of Hassenaah build, who also laid the beams thereof, and set up the doors thereof, the locks thereof, and the bars thereof"* (**Neh. 3:3**).

In **Matthew 4:19**, Jesus told Peter and Andrew

"...Follow me, and I will make you fishers of men".

Thus, **the fish gate** speaks of **evangelism** or winning of souls into God's Kingdom. This gate has been furiously attacked in today's Church. Many Christians have lost the burden for soul winning. Although most Churches are involved in numerous activities and many people seem to "believe" through these activities, those converts only carry the world into the Church. They serve the Lord but also serve their idols. Genuine repentance and getting yoked to Jesus Christ are quite scarce. In fact, in some instances, more people seem to be going out (backsliding) than those coming into Christ.

Satan's attack on the fish gate of the Church is twofold. On the one hand, he has seduced many Churches to lose focus of their primary mission to the world, which is evangelization or the Great Commission. Satan has deceived many to replace evangelization with philanthropic activities. I have seen Christians enthusiastic about making missions trips to the poor countries of the world. However, during these trips, the most they do is give out clothes and food. No sound Gospel is preached in the power of the Holy Spirit, with the intent of calling sinners to the cross of Jesus. Going out there to share food and clothes is very good (and we should do this). However, to only do that and not preach the Gospel which should save the people is to place the cart before the horse.

On the other hand, Satan has sifted some of the bearers of the Good News such that the Word of God in their mouths is nothing but powerless chaffs. In **Jeremiah 23:28**, the Lord said

> *"The prophet that hath a dream, let him tell a dream; and he that hath my word, let him speak my word faithfully. What is the chaff to the wheat? saith the LORD"*

Many prophets today have been sifted and now carry empty dreams which are mere chaffs. Few have the "wheat" of God's Word. Do you remember how Satan sought to have Peter? And ponder this, Satan's intention was not to kill Peter; rather, it was to sift him. Why would Satan, our arch enemy, not seek to kill Peter? This is because Satan is wise and very strategic. He understands that the greatest harm he can do to God's Church is to sift the lives of the people who stand to minister God's Word; to empty Church leaders of the real substance of their lives. Satan understands that if he kills a leader, another person would replace him who may love God better. So, Satan would rather sift a leader and empty him of the treasures of his life. In this way, the leader still occupies his seat but has been emptied. Gradually, God's work suffers and dies under such a leader.

The Church suffers today because many leaders have been sifted. Most have become history in their life time; only telling jokes by the pulpits; only glorying in their past exploits. I have attended evangelistic campaigns of sifted leaders or evangelists. Some 17 years ago, we had an evangelistic campaign. The invited evangelist who preached was very charismatic and popular. However, we learned later on that he slept with a girl at his hotel room who wasn't his wife. These kinds of stories are common nowadays. A Church elder told me at one time that a sister at their Church told him of what transpired when she served as a waitress at a prominent Church growth conference. An evangelist, a person whose ministration apparently shook the conference ground the highest, called the said sister privately and arranged for her to meet with him after the conference. Needless to say the evangelist was a married man. I have attended evangelistic campaigns were the focus was not bringing Christ to lost sinners but rather, the collection of money.

All such practices are indicators of sifted lives. Satan is subtle; he would allow a man in ministry but eat his roots; perforate and syphon the unction from that man. Once this is done, ministry may continue unhindered. However, the fish gate suffers because the unction of the Holy Spirit which should convict and convert sinners is gone.

Friend, our primary purpose on the earth as God's people is to reach the lost with the Gospel. Jesus commanded us

"Therefore go and make disciples in all the nations..." (**Matthew 28:19**, L.B).

This is the meaning of the fish gate. Are you given to evangelism? He who wins souls is wise. Are you a wise Christian? Or are you too busy and entangled with the affairs of this world? We must each arise from our beds of laziness and engage in this ultimate Kingdom business; the winning of souls. We will shine as stars as we so do (**Daniel 12:3**).

THE OLD GATE

*"Moreover the **old gate** repaired Jehoiada the son of Paseah, and Meshullam the son of Besodeiah; they laid the beams thereof, and set up the doors thereof, and the locks thereof, and the bars thereof"* (**Neh. 3:6**).

This gate illustrates the old or ancient paths that God wants us to walk in. The Church of Jesus Christ is not to change with the changing world. In God, there is no variableness or instability (**James 1:17**).

"...His ways are everlasting" (**Habakkuk 3:6**).

This means that His ways are constant and do not change with time, though *methods* may change. If we are truly built on the foundation of the Apostles and Prophets (**Ephesians 2:20**), then we ought to walk in their footsteps. John commanded us to walk in Christ's footsteps as follows

"He that saith he abideth in Him ought himself also so to walk, even as He (Jesus) walked" (**1 John 2:6**).

We are called to

"Be followers of God as dear children" (**Ephesians 5:1**).

However, the old gate has suffered serious attacks from the enemy of God's Church. Many are going around trying to establish their own righteousness. They have zeal, but not based on true knowledge (**Romans 10:1-3**). Even though God said

> "...*Stand ye in the ways, and see, and ask for the old paths, where is the good way, and walk therein, and ye shall find rest for your souls*" (**Jer. 6:16a**),

Yet, the popular response from our generation is

> "...*we will not walk therein*" (**Jeremiah 6:16b**).

Many have forsaken the narrow path of a close walk with the Lord and embraced modern, corrupted Christianity. Many have hewn for themselves broken religious cisterns which can hold no spiritual water. They have stumbled from the ancient paths, having established their own paths.

> "...*they...stumble in their ways from the ancient paths, to walk in paths, in a way not cast up; To make their land desolate, and a perpetual hissing; every one that passeth thereby shall be astonished, and wag his head*" (**Jeremiah 18:15-16**).

The consequence of deviating from the ancient path is desolation and shame. We are in a time of great deception. Another Christ is being presented at several Churches. We look rich physically (with huge cathedrals, expensive cars, private jets, etcetera), but indeed we are poor spiritually. Worldliness and modernism have taken over many Churches. A lot is happening in the Church today which was not so in the beginning.

Divine standards are being lowered in order to make provision for the flesh.

> *"Nevertheless the foundation of God standeth sure, having this seal, The Lord knows them that are His. And, let every one that nameth the name of Christ depart from iniquity"* (**2 Timothy 2:19**).

Many men may drift and follow paths that are not cast up but God's path is sure and unpopular. It is the narrow way that only few can find. Will you continue with the multitudes on the broad way, or will you arise this day

> *"...to defend stoutly the truth which God gave, once for all, to His people to keep without change through the years"* (**Jude 1:3**, L.B).

You see, spiritual warfare is not just binding demons but also battling to defend the truth of God's Word from wolves or false prophets who creep or sneak in or tip-toe into the Church unawares, to sow their tares (**Jude 1:4**). Not many people can notice when false prophets get into the Church. You must be very keen, watchful and spiritually alert to catch them. This is because they speak persuasively and with eloquence, such that the common people are often easily carried away. Why do they sneak in? So that before they are identified, they would have captured many. They are on mission. They turn God's grace into lasciviousness, teaching things of this sort *"Once a person is saved, he is forever saved; for Christ has taken care of our sins; past, present, and future"*. Yet, the Bible warns us in **Romans 11:21** as follows

> *"For if God spared not the natural branches, take heed lest He also spare not thee"*.

These types of prophets of doom have many people following them to their everlasting habitation of hell.

Beloved, the old gate of the Church is a call to return to the beginning and walk with God as Christ, His Apostles and other Church fathers did. Do not join the multitudes today who are purportedly serving the Lord but who have redefined marriage, sin and God's righteous standards. It is not hard to know such folks. Nearly anything you tell them about the need to shun evil and live a holy life before God is interpreted as "legalism". We must strive always, that we may enter through the narrow gate, the old gate; for many will attempt to go in but will be disqualified (**Luke 13:24**).

THE VALLEY GATE

*"The **valley gate** repaired Hanun, and the inhabitants of Zanoah; they built it, and set up the doors thereof, the locks thereof, and the bars thereof..."* (**Neh. 3:13**).

The **valley** represents a place of trial and humiliation. It is a place of lowliness.

"Every valley shall be exalted...." (**Isaiah 40:4**).

The valley gate of the Church speaks of *meekness* and *humility*. These are great treasures that the devil has stolen from many lives. God uses trials to break us and to teach us humility. Therefore, the valley is also the place of trials of our faith. These trials may be so difficult that we even despair of life (**2 Corinthians 1:8**). It could be, as it were, a valley of the shadow of death (**Psalms 23:4**). The Disciples of Christ were willing to follow Him even to death. They did not count their lives dear to them. In **Hebrews 11:35**, we are told that they suffered and refused deliverance from their suffering because such deliverance meant denying their Lord.

Today, however, many in the Church have not the willingness to suffer for Christ. The Christ presented nowadays in several Churches is the Christ without the cross. We are told

> *"For unto you it is given in the behalf of Christ, not only to believe on him, but also to suffer for his sake; Having the same conflict which ye saw in me, and now hear to be in me"* (**Philippians 1:29-30**).

> *"For even hereunto were ye called: because Christ also suffered for us, leaving us an example, that ye should follow his steps"* (**1 Peter 2:21**).

> *"...we must through much tribulation enter into the kingdom of God"* (**Acts 14:22**).

Do you have a readiness to suffer for Christ if it is the Will of God? Suffering or traversing a valley develops meekness, humility, and an attitude of dependence on God in us. God told Israel that He took them through a wilderness journey and fed them with manna for 40 years in order to humble and teach them how to depend on Him, and for them to learn that man should not live by bread alone but by every Word God speaks (**Deuteronomy 8:2-3**). Friend, it is difficult to become truly humble and meek without a valley experience. Some people need many such experiences to truly get broken.

The arrogance, self-reliance, self-promotion, materialism, etcetera prominent in today's Church testify to Satan's work on the valley gate of the Church. The

Church today has more arrogant and boastful people than the truly humble. They boast of their academic attainments, their finances, material possessions, spouses and/or kids, charisma and so on. Others view any trial of their faith as a curse; an indication that one is not walking well with God. I have heard Christians make false or baseless confessions today, such as *"Suffering is not my portion in Jesus' name"*. Such a confession is unbiblical. Our Lord Jesus Christ told us how much we would be hated and persecuted by the world, all for His sake. We don't go about looking for suffering. However, every true Christian must be predisposed to suffer for the sake of Christ. If we suffer with Him, we shall also reign with Him (**Romans 8:17, 2 Timothy 2:12**).

Today, many want an easy path, not the ancient path that goes through the **valley gate**. They are looking for the shortest cuts; results without perspiration. Some would rather sow seeds for quick miracles rather than take up the cross daily to follow the Christ who produces miracles. Yes, meekness and humility are quite scarce today. The increasing divorce rates I mentioned before (and other law suits among Christians) testify to the carnality there is in today's Church. The Bible says we wrestle not against flesh and blood; though we walk in the flesh, yet we war not after the flesh. This means we are not to fight the same way the world fights or with the same carnal weapons the world uses. This isn't true of some Christians today. I have had the privilege of counseling troubled marriages. I have witnessed the flesh at work at such moments. I have heard believers threaten each other with divorce. Some fight after the flesh. Friend, it is a great mistake to view your spouse as your enemy. Satan is the enemy of marriage (he has been from the very beginning). The first marriage God instituted worked well until the day Satan showed up.

Do not fight your spouse; do not fight mere mortals; fight Satan and his elements.

Lack of brokenness in today's Church is a consequence of Satan's attack on the valley gate. When the Apostle Paul reproofed the Corinthian Church on the carnality in their midst, one thing he mentioned was their readiness to drag each other to court. Here is an example of a Church whose valley gate had been destroyed so to speak. Some of today's Christians are very likely to flex their muscles and strike back on any one who dares to step on their toes. They no longer remember Jesus' teaching in **Matthew 5:38-41** which says

> "...resist not evil: but whosoever shall smite thee on thy right cheek, turn to him the other also..."

There are some in today's Church who lack the character of Christ; who prove their strength by retaliation once hurt or taken advantage of; and who have forgotten that the Lord said

> "...avenge not yourselves, but rather give place unto wrath..." (**Romans 12:17-21**).

Such see meek saints as weak people or willing horses for anyone to ride. However, meekness is not weakness but strength under control. A good description of meekness can be seen in **Proverbs 19:11**

> "The discretion of a man deferreth his anger; and it is his glory to pass over a transgression".

You realize that true greatness and strength is in one's ability to control himself and to overlook offences. This is meekness. Meekness is a man's glory. This is why the meek shall inherit the earth (**Matthew 5:5**).

If you do not sense God's full presence and anointing with you, and if you are still so self-defendant, then the **valley gate** of your life has been attacked and demolished by the devil; for God dwells only with the humble.

> *"For thus saith the high and lofty One that inhabiteth eternity, whose name is Holy; I dwell in the high and holy place, with him also that is of a contrite and humble spirit, to revive the spirit of the humble..."* (**Isaiah 57:15**).

THE DUNG GATE

> *"But **the dung gate** repaired Malchiah the son of Rechab, the ruler of part of Beth-haccerem; he built it, and set up the doors thereof, the locks thereof, and the bars thereof"* (**Neh. 3:14**).

The **dung gate** was the gate through which the scapegoat was passed into the wilderness, bearing the sins of the Israelites in the old covenant (**Leviticus 16:7-10**). This gate therefore represents a deep longing for holiness and inner purity. It speaks of a hatred for sin, and a corresponding hunger and thirst for righteousness. It speaks of our continual cleansing from all filthiness of the flesh and of the spirit.

> *"Blessed are they which do hunger and thirst after righteousness: for they shall be filled"* (**Matthew 5:6**).

The enemy has seriously attacked this gate of the Church. Many in the Church have started telling lies, receiving bribes, exaggerating, watching pornography and committing other vile sexual sins, and are addicted to many other sorts of things they never dreamt of when they first believed. Compromise is common nowadays and the inner yearning for holiness has evaporated from several hearts in the Church, including hearts of some gospel ministers. **Sin is no longer the "deadly viper" we knew before, but has been reduced to an ordinary earthworm that anyone can play with**. I heard one of the hyper-grace teachers trivialize sin and mention that Ananias and Sapphira only died in the early Church because they were not truly Disciples of Jesus. Had they been Disciples, they would not have been killed after doing what they did. No kidding beloved. I heard this man speak on TV and sadly, he has many followers. Can you imagine this?

Unfortunately, there are many such preachers and teachers nowadays. Our generation needs tearful preachers who truly have God's fear and who know His terror. Men like the Apostle Paul knew God's terror and spoke against sin bluntly, warning their hearers with many tears (**Acts 20:31 & Phil. 3:18**). Today, we have more of psychological and motivational preachers who laugh and joke when they lightly mention sin once in a while in their sermons. Yet, there is more sin in this generation than any other generation before has ever known. Yes, no exaggeration intended. We live in an evil time.

"Because sentence against an evil work is not executed speedily, therefore the heart of the sons of men is fully set in them to do evil. Though a sinner do evil an hundred times, and his days be prolonged, yet surely

I know that it shall be well with them that fear God, which fear before Him. But it shall not be well with the wicked..." (**Ecclesiastes 8:11-13**).

Men's hearts are set on evil because God delays His judgment in our time. Although God is patient with our generation, this won't go on forever. The Bible says His wrath will come on the children of rebellion or disobedience (**Colossians 3:6**). What is your attitude towards sin? Do you do bad things in the secret, which no one else knows except you and God? Do you hide in your restroom to masturbate? Do you hide in your bedroom to watch pornography and ...? Are you a reprover of all unfruitful works of darkness around you? Are you among the few who sigh daily because of the abominations around them or you delight in sitting in the seat of the scornful and standing in the way of sinners (**Psalms 1:1**)? To "*sit in the seat of the scornful*" is to associate freely with unbelievers and join them in doing things, forgetting that evil communication corrupts good manners. This is the habit of some Christians today. I have heard Christians say "*I cannot trust a believer. I will do business only with non-Christians*". You never hear such Christians pray for a believer's character to be transformed by the Holy Spirit. To "*stand in the way of sinners*" is to take pleasure in watching sinners do the abominable things they do. For example, taking pleasure in watching filthy things over television or attending an orgy not to participate but to watch others. There is tremendous power in vision. The things we set our eyes on will shape us. What you watch, you will either practice it someday or end up with a depraved mind. The things you frequently watch become indelible pictures in your mind and affect your thought life.

The god of this world takes advantage of our vision quite well. Satan is fully behind much of today's fashion designs. Many modern designs for women reveal laps, cleavage and body contours. This is done purposefully. Satan knows that the best way to promote the spirit of lust is to reveal female skin since men are moved by what they see. I was asked to complete a sexual harassment training at my university at one time. At the end of the training, I had to submit a suggestion on how to improve campus life, especially relating to sexual harassment. I mentioned that I felt sexually harassed daily by the "naked" girls allowed on our campus. I added that although I didn't very much like the winter cold, it was a better season because the cold forced women to cover their skin more. How would you forbid men from sexually harassing women, and yet allow those women to seduce men by exposing their bodies? But you see, this is how Satan works. Many of those seducers are his bait.

In modern society, moral standards have gravely deteriorated. Clothes initially meant to be underwear are common attires today. Whereas the idea of shorts for women was a public taboo for many years, girls in modern society now feel free to wear shorts (which are simply too short and too tight) to public places. I was amazed one day when a girl spread herself nearly naked (having on only a G-string) behind my apartment building in the name of wanting to tan her body. As God's people, we need to walk very closely with Jesus to maintain lives of purity. We need to continually cover ourselves, and especially our eyes and minds, with the Blood of Jesus against impure thoughts. Yes, we are new creatures in Christ, but since we still live in a body, we are subject to temptation. Even our Lord Jesus Christ, in the days of His flesh, was tempted in every way as we are, yet without sin.

Let us arise and seek God for the restoration of the **dung gate** of the Church; for many are in the Church who have learned how to shake off the conviction of the Holy Spirit. Some have developed immunity against the Spirit of God!

THE GATE OF THE FOUNTAIN

*"But the **gate of the fountain** repaired Shallun the son of Colhozeh, the ruler of part of Mizpah; he built it, and covered it, and set up the doors thereof, the locks thereof, and the bars thereof..."* (**Neh. 3:15**).

This gate represents the Baptism into the Holy Spirit. When someone gives his/her life to Christ and is Holy Ghost-baptized, a well of spiritual water (the Holy Spirit with His wonderful fruit and other effects) starts off in that life, which should increase as the person makes spiritual progress until it becomes a fountain for his/her thirsty surrounding to drink. A fountain is actually an outburst of water, which is what happens when one is baptized into the Holy Spirit.

This is confirmed by what Jesus said in **John 4:14**

"But whosoever drinketh of the water that I shall give him shall never thirst; but the water that I shall give him shall be in him a well of water springing up into everlasting life".

Also in **Isaiah 41:17-18**, God promised to open rivers in the high places and fountains in the valleys for the poor and needy to drink. **The gate of the fountain** therefore speaks of the believer in Christ staying fresh, satisfied (after being filled with the Holy Spirit) and being able also to satisfy the longing of his poor, needy and thirsty world.

However, you will agree that this is not actually a full reality in our time. Most believers today actually look thirsty and needy themselves. How can thirsty and spiritually needy people quench the thirst of others? Some in our Churches are prisoners of hope (as **Zechariah 9:12** puts it); spiritually poor and naked; and look like captives who themselves need deliverance. This may look a little odd but is the sad truth. I have been to meetings where Christians would cry and respond to Altar calls for deliverance prayers. There is no problem with responding to an Altar call for prayer. The problem is when the same believers respond to such prayers over and over and yet, remain apparently bound.

A Church with a healthy fountain gate is a Church filled with the Holy Spirit and continual times of refreshing. Restoring this gate will quench the thirst of many in the Church and bring contentment. What are you thirsty for? Many are thirsty for the things of this world. They are rushing after money, cars, houses, careers and so on. The Lord Jesus asked us to seek first God's Kingdom righteousness. Many have reversed the order today and are seeking mundane things.

The restlessness and desire for earthly things in many lives is an indication of destroyed fountain gates. For Jesus promised that if anyone drinks of the water of the Holy Spirit, he/she would thirst no longer. What do you have for your generation? Are you issuing out sweet and bitter waters at the same time? Are you using your mouth to bless God and curse people at the same time? The Bible says

> "The mouth of a righteous man is a well of life: but violence covereth the mouth of the wicked. The tongue of

*the just is as choice silver: the heart of the wicked is of lit-
tle worth. The lips of the righteous feed many: but fools
die for want of wisdom"* (**Proverbs 10:11, 20, 21**).

Do your lips feed many? A lot of people are in the
church with raw tongues. Wherever they go, someone is
likely to be wounded or hurt by what they say.

The devil has stopped the wells of many lives just
as the Philistines did with the wells Abraham dug and
left for his son Isaac **(Genesis 26:15-18).** You have to do
to the fountain gate of your life exactly what Isaac did
to the wells the Philistines had blocked. You have to dig
again, and importunate God for the Blessed Holy Spirit.

THE WATER GATE

*"Moreover the Nethinims dwelt in Ophel, unto the
place over against **the water gate** toward the east,
and the tower that lieth out"* (**Neh. 3:26**).

The true disciple of Jesus Christ is not supposed to
end at the level of issuing out only a fountain of spiritual waters but ought to grow to the point of releasing
mighty torrents. Thus, the **water gate** is different from
the gate of the fountain in that it has to do with mighty
rivers flowing out of the mature disciple with the pow-
erful effect of eroding all filth and breaking obstacles
in the surroundings. You will agree with me that water current or force in a river is much stronger than in
a fountain. Whereas the fountain quenches thirst and
brings freshness into the environment, the river erodes
and breaks yokes or obstacles in accordance with **Isaiah
10:27** which says

"And it shall come to pass in that day, that his bur-
den shall be taken away from off thy shoulder, and his
yoke from off thy neck, and the yoke shall be destroyed
because of the anointing".

Jesus promised rivers flowing through the mature
believer in **John 7:37-39**

"...He that believeth on me, as the scripture hath
saith, out of his belly shall flow rivers of living water.
(But this spake he of the Spirit...)".

He made this declaration at **the Feast of Tabernacles** which is the seventh feast of the Lord observed by
the Israelites. The spiritual symbolism of this feast is *maturity*. The feast of tabernacles is the feast of maturity.
This feast was often filled with bliss and thankfulness.
The fact that Jesus made the offer in **John 7:37-39** at the
feast of maturity may indicate that spiritual rivers are
not expected to flow out of novices or babes in Christ,
but have to do with maturity. This is why God promises
to open rivers only in high places; that is, among the
mature

"I will open rivers in high places, and fountains in the
midst of the valleys:.." (**Isaiah 41:18**).

Rivers are for high places and not for low land areas among spiritually immature folks. These rivers are
meant for the liberation of captives. Contrarily, fountains are in the plains where children in the faith dwell.
I hope you recall the Apostle John's classification of the
Church into children, young men and fathers?

When we look at today's Church, it is apparent that
the water gate has suffered serious attacks from the evil

one as many captives can be seen amidst the Daughter of Zion. As I ponder, I can only join Jeremiah, the Prophet, to ask

> *"Behold the voice of the cry of the daughter of my people because of them that dwell in a far country: Is not the Lord in Zion? is not her king in her? Why have they provoked me to anger with their graven images, and with strange vanities? The harvest is past, the summer is ended, and we are not saved. For the hurt of the daughter of my people am I hurt; I am black; astonishment hath taken hold on me. Is there no balm in Gilead; is there no physician there? why then is not the health of the daughter of my people recovered?"* **(Jeremiah 8:19-22)**

> *"Is Israel a servant? is he a homeborn slave? why is he spoiled?"* **(Jeremiah 2:14)**

In several respects, the Daughter of Zion has been wounded. Her wound is perpetual and she's been spoiled. We truly need the anointing that will break every yoke in our midst as God's people. We need the water gate of the Church restored. Arise with me, and knock at the water gate. If Jesus says

> *"...knock and it shall be opened unto you"* **(Matthew 7:7)**,

it is because there are spiritual gates for us to knock at. Let us pray that water will again flow from the Lord's temple as in **Ezekiel Chapter 47**.

THE HORSE GATE

*"From above the **horse gate** repaired the priests, every one over against his house"* (**Neh. 3:28**).

Jesus Christ will return to the earth riding on a white horse,

"And I saw heaven opened, and behold a white horse; and He that sat upon him was called Faithful and True, and in righteousness he doth judge and make war" (**Revelation 19:11**).

This speaks of victory and dominion. We are called to be more than conquerors according to **Romans 8:37**. This is the meaning of the horse gate. The horse gate of the Church speaks of our walking in God's Might; having authority over life's adverse circumstances. Think of Christ's authority over death and over natural forces such as the storm at sea. **Romans 5:17** speaks of us reigning in life through Jesus Christ, while **Romans 16:20** speaks of God crushing Satan from under our feet. The horse gate refers to those Christians who, through the abundance of grace provided in Christ Jesus, do reign in life; having Satan under their feet at all times.

Reigning in life is a promised made to all believers in Christ, not a select few, as we find Jesus Himself declaring

"Behold, I give unto you power to tread on serpents and scorpions, and over all the power of the enemy: and nothing shall by any means hurt you" (**Luke 10:19**)

"And these signs shall follow them that believe; In my name shall they cast out devils; they shall speak with new tongues" (**Mark 16:17**),

When the horse gate of the Church is restored, the job of pastors or shepherds of God's flock will reduce greatly. Many sheep who are constantly going to their pastors for prayers who have dominion and do the work of an evangelist, saving other souls. A Church with a healthy horse gate is a Church wherein, members tread on serpents and scorpions, and over ALL the power of the enemy (Satan). Unfortunately, **Mark 16:17** has been reduced in many lives to mere speaking in empty tongues which cannot frighten or scare away "a fly". Many have lost spiritual authority and have been subjugated by demons and/or circumstances.

King Solomon spoke of a folly in his time which seems to repeat itself in our generation.

"Folly is set in great dignity, and the rich sit in low place. I have seen servants upon horses, and princes walking as servants upon the earth" (**Ecclesiastes 10:6-7**).

Princes who ought to be riding on horses are going on foot as servants to opposing forces of darkness and circumstances of life. Let us arise and knock at the horse gate until it is opened. We must fully represent our Master, Jesus Christ, on the earth; for Jesus is building His Church and the gates of hell shall not prevail against it.

THE EAST GATE

"After them repaired Zadok the son of Immer over against his house. After him repaired also Shemaiah

*the son of Shechaniah, the keeper of the **east gate***"
(**Neh. 3:29**).

The **east gate** is the gate by which Jesus Christ comes
into His Church. You see, spiritual gates are very important. The Lord does not just come in anyhow but has
a gate through which He comes into the Church and our
lives. Let's confirm this from the following passages in
the book of **Ezekiel 43 & 44**.

*"Afterward He brought me to the gate, even the gate
that looketh toward the east: And behold, the glory
of the God of Israel came from the way of the east:
and His voice was like a noise of many waters: and
the earth shined with His glory. And the glory of the
Lord came into the house by the way of the gate whose
prospect is toward the east"* (**Ezekiel 43:1,2,4**).

*"Then He brought me back the way of the gate of the
outward sanctuary which looketh toward the east;
and it was shut. Then said the Lord unto me; This
gate shall be shut, it shall not be opened, and no man
shall enter in by it; because the Lord, the God of Israel, hath entered in by it, therefore it shall be shut"*
(**Ezekiel 44:1-2**).

The spiritually dry atmosphere in many Churches,
devoid of God's presence, is an evidence of the destruction of the east gate. Yes, our Lord is yet to enter into
some Churches. In **Revelation 3:20**, we read of a Church
which did not have the presence of God in it; Jesus
stood at the door to that Church, knocking. Similarly,
the absence of God's presence and glory in a Christian
is a sign that the east gate of the concerned has been broken down. When this happens, a person could go into

prayers and spend hours without sensing God's presence or experiencing a break through. This is why some
go to Church and even when the coordinator or minister
encourages worshippers in words of the sort "*Let us get
into the Spirit*", they still can't get into the Spirit. You see,
you cannot really get into the Spirit. Rather, if you keep
the east gate of your life opened, Jesus comes in freely
by the Holy Spirit. The Lord Himself taught us how to
keep our east gates opened. He said

> "*...If a man loves me, he will keep my words: and my
> Father will love him, and we will come unto him, and
> make our abode with him*" (**John 14:23**).

When you fail to keep His Word, you are closing
your **east gate** and no matter how hard you try to get
into the Spirit, you will not succeed. We need to cry out
until the **east gate** is restored through the obedience of
the Saints to God's infallible Word. Obedience to God
and submission to spiritual authority will open our
east gates for the glory of God to fill our lives, and the
Church as was the case in the days of Solomon, the king.
When the Ark of God was brought into the temple in
the days of Solomon, the glory of the Lord so filled the
temple that the priests could not stand to minister.

> "*...then the house was filled with a cloud, even the
> house of the Lord; So that the priests could not stand to
> minister by reason of the cloud: for the glory of the Lord
> had filled the house of God*" (**2 Chronicles 5:13-14**).

When God's glory is absent in a Church, men are
the ones ministering. You would hear some say "this is
my church", "this is my ministry", "these are my sheep"
and so on. When God, however, fills His Church, men

give way to Him to minister to His flock! Let us join the Psalmist to command the east gate to be opened so that the King of Glory may come into His Church and feed His flock (using earthen vessels).

> *"Lift up your heads, O ye gates; and be ye lift up, ye everlasting doors; and the King of glory shall come in. Who is this King of glory? The Lord strong and mighty, the Lord mighty in battle. Lift up your heads, O ye gates; even lift them up, ye everlasting doors; and the King of glory shall come in. Who is this King of glory? The Lord of hosts, He is the King of glory"* (**Psalms 24:7-10**).

THE GATE MIPHKAD

> *"After him repaired Malchiah the goldsmith's son unto the place of the Nethinims, and of the merchants, over against the **gate Miphkad**, and to the going up of the corner"* (**Neh. 3:31**).

An online Jewish encyclopedia defines the Hebrew word *miphkad* as *"the appointment place"* or *"the hall of judgment"*. Therefore, the miphkad gate speaks of judgment. The Apostle Paul said

> *"For we must all appear before the judgment seat of Christ; that every one may receive the things done in his body, according to that he hath done, whether it be good or bad"* (**2 Corinthians 5:10**)

We must each live with this understanding of coming judgment. We will render account of our lives before God. None is exempt from this. This consciousness helps us examine or judge ourselves daily as the Scriptures say in **1 Corinthians 11:31** and **2 Corinthians 13:5**.

Some Christians have been deceived into believing that Christians or believers won't be judged. This is not true. In His parables, Jesus showed us that the works of believers would be examined or judged. This is seen, for example, in the parable of the talents. In **Revelation 3:2**, the Lord Jesus told a Church that He hadn't found her works perfect before His Father. This suggests that He had weighed those works and closely examined them. Remember that the Father Himself judges no one but has committed all judgment to His Son, our Master Jesus Christ (**John 5:22**). Every man's work shall be tested by fire, to prove its quality (**1 Corinthians 3:13-15**). God is no respecter of persons; He favors no one. He is a just God who will reward each of us according to our deeds.

Knowing this, we must work out our salvation with fear and trembling. This fear is not in many hearts in today's Church. Many nowadays neither tremble at God's Word nor fear to violate His principles. Yet, the Apostle Peter warned

> "For the time is come that judgment must begin at the house of God: and if it first begin at us, what shall the end be of them that obey not the gospel of God? And if the righteous scarcely be saved, where shall the ungodly and the sinner appear?" (**1 Peter 4:17-18**).

Much of today's preaching falls short of warning people of coming judgment; it fails to call sin for what it is and urge sinners to repent. God told Isaiah

> "Cry aloud, spare not, lift up thy voice like a trumpet, and shew my people their transgression, and the house of Jacob their sins" (**Isaiah 58:1**).

We need preachers today who can cry aloud, without sparing anything but calling out all sin, raising their voices as a trumpet, and bringing conviction upon sinners. No one can become this kind of preacher without truly knowing God's terror. When we know God's terror, we would preach with so much passion, as did the apostle Paul.

Sadly, the cultures of this world have helped shape Christianity for the worst. Most parents, for example, (including Christian parents) have lost the grip over their children because they won't discipline them according to God's Word. The society has given rights which go to extremes. Many kids grow up in the United States today without getting flogged once by their parents although they could be naughty and commit many crimes worthy of flogging. Flogging a child to correct and train up that child to go the right way is not sinful. The much freedom we have in our modern society makes it hard to rebuke someone of sin in their lives. Church discipline, that is, placing some form of disciplinary restrictions on a Church member who sins, is very rare in the United States nowadays. In most of our Churches, people are free to live just any kind of life and yet attend Church. It is not uncommon to find Church folks addicted to drugs or alcohol, cohabiting or living in sexual sin, get babies out of wedlock and have the Church organize baby showers rather than frown at the sin, and so on. All of these indicate that the miphkad gate of the Church has been destroyed and our sense of judgment has been lost.

Conclusion

Let me bring out one more truth as we conclude this chapter. The arrangement of these gates is quite significant because it reflects the spiritual progress of a Christian. In order for sinners to be saved, there must be a healthy **sheep gate** with genuine ministers bringing to them the Word of God and getting them saved through the **fish gate**. These new believers must then walk in the ancient path of the Apostles (**the old gate**) if they are to abide in Christ; their characters being developed through the **valley gate.** In all these, they must continue to long more and more for inner purity (**the dung gate**). This will lead to fountains of living water flowing out of their lives (**the gate of the fountain** or **baptism into the Holy Spirit**) ultimately becoming rivers (**the water gate**). You notice where the fountain and water gates appear. It is after character formation. This is the authentic anointing. The Christians will then fully walk in spiritual authority (**the horse gate**) experiencing the shekina glory of God by way of the **East gate**; walking in total submission to God, being mindful of His justice and judgment by way of the **Miphkad gate**.

CHAPTER THREE

THE SEVEN CHURCHES OF ASIA MINOR

The message of the Lord Jesus Christ to the seven Churches in Asia Minor is quite revealing and worthy of special note as we seek to fully understand the state of the Church today and what we have lost. Although Bible scholars largely hold that these seven Churches picture the different dispensations of the Church Age, the Churches in our time can be grouped into seven categories represented by the Churches in **Revelations 2 & 3**. Indeed, viewing the messages to these Churches as representative of the phases of the Church Age or descriptors of the frames into which one Church or the other in our time may fit really makes no difference. The key issue is that a close examination of these messages sheds further light on what the Church has lost.

Again, it is important for us to fully understand the state of the Church, and that of our lives, so that we can properly cry for restoration. A clear understanding of what it is that we are to pursue in seeking restoration is an important prerequisite for effectively praying for revival and restoration. Multitudes came to Jesus but only seeking meat which perishes (**John 6:25-27**). They knew not of the meat which endures eternally. Seeking Jesus is one thing and doing so with the right intentions is quite another. Our prayers cannot be effectual unless we understand what we are crying for. We will now move on to analyze the message of our Lord Jesus Christ to the seven Churches in Asia Minor.

THE CHURCH IN EPHESUS

"Unto the angel of the church of Ephesus write; These things saith He that holdeth the seven stars in His right hand, who walketh in the midst of the seven golden candlesticks; I know thy works, and thy labour and thy patience, and how thou cannot bear them which are evil: and thou has tried them which say they are apostles, and are not, and has found them liars: And has borne, and has patience, and for my name's sake has laboured, and has not fainted. Nevertheless I have somewhat against thee, because thou has left thy first love. Remember therefore from whence thou art fallen, and repent, and do the first works; or else I will come unto thee quickly, and will remove thy candlestick out of his place, except thou repent. But this thou has, that thou hatest the deeds of the Nicolaitans, which I also hate. He that hath an ear, let him hear what the Spirit saith unto the churches; To him that overcometh will I give to eat of the tree of life, which is in the midst of the paradise of God" (**Rev. 2:1-7**).

The Lord Jesus Christ praised the Church in Ephesus on the following qualities:

- Their labor
- Their patience
- Their ability to test and resist evil, false teachings (e.g., the teachings of the Nicolaitans), and false teachers or apostles or prophets

- Their fortitude and ability to face adversity without fainting

Thus, it may be said that the Ephesian Church was zealous for the Lord. When we look at these virtues, we understand that they form part of what the Lord is looking for in His Church. When the Lord Jesus Christ looks at His Church, He desires to see each of us laboring relentlessly, not in worldly pursuits but for His purposes (and with Him); He desires to see us exercise patience and face every challenging circumstance with faith; He expects us to resist evil, test and identify false prophets.

When we look at today's Church (and our individual lives), it may be said that most Churches lack the above virtues. In the average American Church, for example, service to the Lord and the people is limited to a few who are on the Church's payroll. In most cases, ministry is seen just like any other job, rather than as a Divine Call. It is very common for Churches nowadays to hire paid musicians to play music at their services. The Church has lost that sense of selfless service and passion wherein, every saved person desires to labor for the Lord free of charge.

On false doctrines, most Churches nowadays are open to accepting the opinions of men in lieu of the truth of God's Word. Many have not the sense of discernment to be able to try and prove false apostles and prophets. I went to a Church and a hyper-grace guest speaker spoke at the Church that morning. Of course, he said many things which were off balance and the Holy Spirit in me was very grieved. After the message, however, the Bishop of the Church went to the pulpit to praise the preacher and his message; adding insults to injury, so to speak.

We live in the perilous times and most Christians lack the fortitude to endure hardness as faithful soldiers of the cross of Jesus. For example, many have no time trusting God for provision in their time of need, they would rather turn to credit card companies. Many also have no time waiting on the Lord for healing; they would rather turn to their health insurance and physicians. In **2 Chronicles 16:12-13**, we find that king Asa of Judah took ill and sought the physicians instead of the Lord. He died consequently. While God does work in diverse ways, including using physicians to heal, we must put God first in all situations; we must seek Him in every crisis first. Without God's intervention, health insurance or good medical care won't keep a person alive.

The Ephesian Church corresponds to Churches today full of labors of good works for the Lord, patient endurance, discipline and hatred of all that God hates. As a human, I would think a Church in this category is excellent; being filled with godliness and zeal for the Lord. In the Lord's eyes, however, they lack one thing; *"they have left their first love"*.

You see, one could do a thousand good things and yet, fail to meet love's needs! Here was a Church recommended for many good works, none of which could substitute or make up for the **"first love"** Married couples should take note. Love has particular **keys**. Find out the keys to your partner's heart (some have referred to this as "the love language"). If you fail to do this, you could be doing your best and yet he/ she feels nothing.

Let us all find out the keys to God's heart too. God needs love just as we humans do. This is why the first and greatest commandment is to love Him with the whole heart, soul, mind and strength. Do you still have deep love and passion for Christ and His Word as before, or has your zeal dwindled over the years? Are you still committed to prayer, giving, evangelism etc, as before or have idols invaded your life? Demas who worked zealously with Paul later on loved the world

> *"For Demas hath forsaken me, having loved this present world…"* (**2 Timothy 4:10**).

You see, if you have left your first love, it could only mean that other things have taken over your heart. No vacuum exists in real life. A heart devoid of God's love is filled with the love of this world. We note that good religious activities do not substitute for the "first love" God is seeking from each of us. That you are laboring for God and resisting evil to the shedding of blood doesn't automatically imply that you love God passionately. In marriage, a wife may be excellent at the kitchen, in taking care of her husband's clothes and other things, and in other household chores. However, if she doesn't spend time with her husband and offer him her body, the man may still not feel her love. The same applies to excellent husbands who do not understand the keys to their wives' hearts. Also for the Lord, zeal in good works doesn't make Him feel our love. We need to pant for Him; spend time with Him; and desire to do His Will always. Correct ministry originates from our love and passion for the Lord. The Lord Jesus asked Peter thrice if he loved Him. Only on the basis of that love did He charge Peter to feed His sheep.

THE CHURCH IN SMYRNA

> *"And unto the angel of the church in Smyrna write; These things saith the first and the last, which was dead, and is alive; I know thy works, and tribulation,*

and poverty, (but thou art rich) and I know the blas-
phemy of them which say they are Jews, and are not,
but are the synagogue of Satan. Fear none of those
things which thou shalt suffer: behold, the devil shall
cast some of you into prison, that ye may be tried;
and ye shall have tribulation ten days: be thou faithful
unto death, and I will give thee a crown of life. He
that hath an ear, let him hear what the Spirit saith
unto the churches; He that overcometh shall not be
hurt of the second death" (**Rev. 2:8-11**).

The Church in Smyrna had most qualities praised
in the Ephesian Church. The Christians at Smyrna did
suffer and endured much persecution for righteousness
and Christ's sake. They were slandered by false prophets and suffered many things from the heathen and
false brethren. They were economically poor (like most
Churches in third world countries are nowadays). However, they were rich spiritually and apparently resisted
false apostles (the Lord mentioned knowing those of the
Synagogue of Satan, suggesting these were likely not in
the fold of the Saints).

Smyrna represents Churches which are spiritually rich but economically poor. Apparently, we find no
rebuke from the Lord to the Church in Smyrna. I once
was a part of a village Church in my country in Africa.
The building was partially dilapidated, with unplas-
tered walls and a dusty floor. We had a few wooden
benches and our Church was under 50 members. Yet,
God's presence was so real in that Church. I have not
witnessed such a Divine presence in any of the American Churches I've been to. I have seen firsthand what it
means to be poor physically but rich spiritually. Having
been a devout Christian in Africa and in the U.S.A., I

can testify that the Church in the United States has gone much deeper into compromise or worldliness. The reverse is true when comparing physical riches.

While physical riches are good, spiritual riches are much better. If we seek the Lord and offer ourselves to do His Will, He will add to us many other things we need for life here on earth. Sadly, many Christians today suppose that "...*gain is godliness...*" (**1 Timothy 6:5**). Consequently, their labors are not directed at seeking the Lord and His righteousness but at gaining earthly riches. The gospel today has been destroyed by greed or the love of money. It's a shame how most of us have become so beggarly. Some preachers are now selling miracles, anointing oil, anointing water, special jewelries and so on. One hardly listens to a message on Christian TV nowadays without being told to sow a seed for a miracle. We suggest to the world that we serve a God who is not able, and whose favors must be bought with money (so contrary to Biblical teachings). Much of today's doctrine suggests that being poor is a curse. But God has chosen the poor to be rich in faith,

> *"Hearken, my beloved brethren, Hath not God chosen the poor of this world rich in faith, and heirs of the kingdom which He hath promised to them that love Him?"* (**James 2:5**).

The Lord holds nothing against Churches like the Church in Smyrna. He only encourages them to stand firm in persecution to the end. We do not hear Jesus saying "I have this against you, that you are poor". It is possible (but difficult) to be materially rich and at the same time, fully yielded to the Lord. The physically rich often fall into diverse temptations

"But they that will be rich fall into temptation and a snare, and into many foolish and hurtful lusts, which drown men in destruction and perdition" **(1 Timothy 6:9).**

The Word of God does not tell lies. The above scripture is true and cannot be twisted. Without sounding like an advocate for poverty, I agree with God's Word that the pursuit of earthly riches is a slippery slope. The Laodicean Church was physically rich and failed to satisfy the heart of the Lord Jesus Christ. We will see this later. Likewise, many western Churches are materially rich but spiritually destitute, being given to pleasure.

THE CHURCH IN PERGAMOS

"And to the angel of the church in Pergamos write; These things saith he which hath the sharp sword with two edges; I know thy works, and where thou dwellest, even where Satan's seat is: and thou holdest fast my name, and hast not denied my faith, even in those days wherein Antipas was my faithful martyr, who was slain among you, where Satan dwelleth. But I have a few things against thee, because thou hast there them that hold the doctrine of Balaam, who taught Balak to cast a stumbling block before the children of Israel, to eat things sacrificed unto idols, and to commit fornication. So hast thou also them that hold the doctrine of the Nicolaitans, which thing I hate. Repent; or else I will come unto thee quickly, and will fight against them with the sword of my mouth. He that hath an ear, let him hear what the Spirit saith unto the churches; To him that overcometh will I give to eat of the hidden manna, and will give him a white stone, and in the

stone a new name written, which no man knoweth saving he that receiveth it" (**Rev. 2:12-17**).

This frame fits those Churches which are a mix of faithful believers and those holding false teachings. Some Church leaders use the Parable of the Tares (**Matthew 13:24-30, 36-43**) as a justification for allowing members who are like "tares" in their Churches. But in interpreting this parable, Jesus stated that the field where Satan planted tares is "the world", not "the Church" (**Matthew 13:38**). If one views these tares as growing in the Church with the Lord asking that they be allowed to grow, then Church discipline and ex-communication as taught in passages like **Matthew 18:15-18** and **1 Corinthians 5:1-13** would be meaningless. Whereas many Churches nowadays have "tares" in their midst, this is not God's ideal. As Paul warned the Church in Corinth not to maintain fellowship with false disciples, so did he charge Timothy to openly rebuke those who sinned in the Church, in order to instill fear in other members (**1 Timothy 5:20**).

Pergamos represents Churches which are a mixture of good and bad. I used to watch a popular Christian TV channel here in the U.S.A. This channel is a good example of Pergamos. At one moment, the channel would air or broadcast a good theologically balanced message. At another moment, a hyper-grace preacher would come up to preach heresy. I stopped watching this channel. It seemed that those managing it couldn't discern or distinguish light from darkness; truth from heresy.

The Lord's warning to Pergamos involved rebukes on the doctrines of Balaam and the Nicolaitans. It behooves us to briefly examine these doctrines. While Balaam might have been a prophet of God at one time, he certainly was backslidden at the time of his encounter with Balak, king of Moab (**Numbers 22-24**). That he was being hired by the heathen to cast spells on their enemies suggests that Balaam was backslidden, had he been a true prophet before. Moreover, he had developed his own doctrine which the Lord Jesus Christ condemned in the Church in Pergamos. I do not want to dwell much on the person of Balaam. I want to focus on "the doctrine of Balaam" or "the way of Balaam" – **2 Peter 2:15**. Balaam advised Balak to send beautiful Moabite women into the camp of Israel to seduce them to commit sexual immorality with them. He also advised Balak on how to seduce Israel to worship the idols of Moab. In **Numbers 31:15-16**, we read

> "*And Moses said unto them, Have ye saved all the women alive? Behold, these caused the children of Israel, through the counsel of Balaam, to commit trespass against the Lord in the matter of Peor, and there was a plague among the congregation of the Lord*".

The counsel of Balaam led Israel to compromise their faith in God by idolatry and sexual immorality with Moabite women. Balaam was a man driven by greed (**Jude 1:11**). He loved the wages of unrighteousness (**2 Peter 2:15**). Any Church with ministers who are greedy for money and love the wages of unrighteousness fits the Church in Pergamos. Let me give two examples of the attitude of godly people towards money and material things. Abraham refused gifts from the king of Sodom because he was ungodly (i.e., he would later boast for making Abraham rich) – **Genesis 14:23**. Elisha likewise refused gifts from Naaman who was a heathen **2 Kings 5:1-19**. Contrarily, many Gospel ministers today are quick to accept gifts (especially money), without bothering about the sources of such gifts. The offerings of a human trafficker or drug dealer or prostitute would be accepted easily in most of today's Churches. In fact, the "fat" offerings or tithes of such people could even lead to their being promoted to the offices of deacon or elder. Leadership appointments at some Churches nowadays are mediated by the wealth of the individuals involved and how well they give to the Church. All such Churches and greedy ministers have gone the way of Balaam and fit the Pergamos frame.

The Doctrine of Balaam promotes idolatry, immorality, the trading of God's Word for money (**2 Cor. 2:17**), and partial obedience to God's Word (which is, of course, total rebellion). When Balaam failed to give Balak the true Word of God, he ended up giving Balak his own ideas. The Doctrine of Balaam replaces the Word of God with the ideas of men. Some today argue that the Bible is not the full revelation about God. They use Scriptures like **John 21:25** which states that many things Jesus did are unwritten. Such have gone the way of Balaam. We know, however, that the Bible is the full revelation about God because what is unwritten cannot negate or contradict any of what is written.

We now turn to the *"doctrine of the Nicolaitains"*. The name "Nicolaitane" is derived from a combination of three Greek words; *"nikos"* meaning *"to conquer"*, *"laicos"* meaning *"laymen"*, and *"ton"* meaning *"the"*. Therefore *"Nicolaitane"* could be translated literally as *"to conquer the laymen"*. This is very much similar to the leaven of the Pharisees against which, the Lord Jesus warned His disciples. The Pharisees exalted themselves to a completely higher pedestal than any other person who heard them. They were described as proud and desirous of respect/ honor, and the praises of men. The Doctrine of the Nicolaitans is embedded in this. This doctrine projects the clergy above the laymen or Christians in the pews. I remember when I first got saved, I didn't believe a pastor can sin. This was because of the way we viewed our pastors; we thought they were perfect people who were quite close to God (and yes, a good shepherd ought indeed to be close to the Chief Shepherd, the Lord Jesus Christ). Contrary to Christ's teaching on His servants learning of His meekness and humility as they feed His sheep, the doctrine of the Nicolaitans exalts the clergy above the laity, and virtually sees the former as "lords".

While the Church in Ephesus hated the deeds of the Nicolaitans (**Revelation 2:6**), Pergamos embraced them. Today, there are Churches which have embraced the most gruesome sinful practices to the extent of allowing sinners yoked in such vile sins to serve as their priests or ministers. There are also Churches which treat their ministers as demi gods who are "untouchable" or cannot be called to question. This is especially true of some ministry founders. I recall viewing one minister being carried by his Church members as a king. Oh, how disgusting it is when men take God's place in the Church. All such are they who hold the doctrine of the Nicolaitans; which thing, the Lord hates.

All those who entertain the doctrines of Balaam and the Nicolaitans must repent and turn to the Lord. Otherwise, Christ promises to be an enemy to them and to fight against them with the sword of His mouth (i.e., His undefiled Word which challenges false doctrine). To fight against false prophets, you need the sword of Jesus' mouth, which is the Word of God. In our Church, we do a lot of teaching because we believe that false teachings can only be counteracted by the truth of God's Word. Therefore we labor to fully equip our members with God's Truth.

THE CHURCH IN THYATIRA

"And unto the angel of the church in Thyatira write; These things saith the Son of God, who hath His eyes like unto a flame of fire, and his feet are like fine brass; I know thy works, and charity, and service, and faith, and thy patience, and thy works; and the last to be more than the first. Notwithstanding I have a few things against thee, because thou sufferest that woman Jezebel, which calleth herself a prophetess, to teach and to seduce my servants to commit fornication, and to eat things sacrificed unto idols. And I gave her space to repent of her fornication; and she repented not. Behold, I will cast her into a bed, and them that commit adultery with her into great tribulation, except they repent of their deeds. And I will kill her children with death; and all the churches shall know that I am He which searcheth the reins and hearts: and I will give unto every one of you according to your works" (**Rev. 2:18-23**).

Thyatira represents Churches which are much like Pergamos; a mixture of good and evil. These Churches still have elements of brotherly love, faith, patience and Christian service, but have been conquered by *"the spirit of Jezebel"*. The spirit of Jezebel is the spirit of idolatry, sexual immorality, worldliness and sensuality. To know a little more about this demon, let's briefly look at the character of the wicked queen Jezebel.

"Now therefore send, and gather to me all Israel unto mount Carmel, and the prophets of Baal four hundred and fifty, and the prophets of the groves four hundred, which eat at Jezebel's table" (**1 Kings 18:19**).

Notice that Jezebel was a queen of idolatry. She controlled and fed the prophets of the idols in Israel. Once the spirit of Jezebel takes hold of a Church, idols are introduced. I remember meeting a couple who told me they left one Church because idolatry entered the Church and a Sunday evening evangelistic service the Church used to hold was replaced with football. When idolatry sets in, the things of this world take God's place; Church members would stay away from Church because of worldly commitments; Church members would rather go watch football or a movie than attend a Church prayer meeting or go witnessing.

"But there was none like unto Ahab, which did sell himself to work wickedness in the sight of the Lord, whom Jezebel his wife stirred up" (**1 Kings 21:25**).

You notice again that Jezebel was also a queen of great wickedness and quite influential. She ruled her husband indirectly. She manipulated and stirred up Ahab towards evil. This is one serious element of the spirit of Jezebel. This spirit manifests in women who seek to lord it over their husbands and who strive to be equal with men. Female insubordination to male authority, according to God's design, is rooted in the spirit of Jezebel. God's principles teach women to be in subjection to their own husbands even if those husbands are not in the faith (**1 Peter 3:1-6**). Sarah obeyed Abraham, calling him *lord*. See the contrast between Sarah and Jezebel. Jezebel indirectly ruled the kingdom. King Ahab's seal was in her keeping and she could write letters at any time with any content in his name, seal and circulate and the king would do nothing about it (**1 Kings 21:8-16**). Ahab feared Jezebel. Dear sister, is your husband afraid of you? Does your husband tremble when you speak? There is a saying here in the United States which goes as follows to women "Do you wear the pants in your home?". This statement usually implies "are you the one in charge of your home rather than your husband?" There are women with tremendous evil influence on the lives of their husbands and the ministries committed to them by the Lord. Right in the Garden of Eden, we find elements of the spirit of Jezebel when Eve led her husband into evil. After meeting with Satan, Eve became Adam's head or leader, leading him into sin. The spirit of Jezebel always seeks manipulation or control. This spirit always wants to be in charge; it always wants to be the "teaching prophetess" in a Church. Behind all feminist ideologies is the spirit of Jezebel. Satan is a usurper of authority and works to stir rebellion against all forms of authority on earth, including women usurping authority over men.

> "And when Jehu was come to Jezreel, Jezebel heard of it; **and she painted her face, and attired her head,** and looked out at a window" (**2 Kings 9:30**).

Thus, the spirit of Jezebel is also associated with paintings or wearing of sensual makeups. David Pack, founder and overseer of The Restored Church of God, writing on *The Truth Hidden Behind Makeup* states as follows

> "The first women to wear makeup were prostitutes! Changing one's appearance by facial paint is a custom ancient prostitutes have dictated to the modern age. Cosmetics were nothing more than a device used by harlots to, in effect, teach men to break the Seventh Commandment. This is the message of history – yet the whole world lies in ignorance of these facts! ...At

the turn of the twentieth century, makeup was viewed
as something only proud, even arrogant women wore.
With the invention of movies and television, Holly-
wood injected into the limelight the image of a movie
starlet's face covered with cosmetics. Once this image
was accepted by the masses, cosmetics became com-
monplace".

Whereas sensual makeup is now common even in
the Church, it was widely a worldly practice among
prostitutes for a long time. The Bible does not state Jezebel's motive in painting her face and making up her
hair before looking at Jehu. Could she possibly have
been seeking to seduce Jehu? Jezebel was an idolatress
and most likely an adulteress too (a widow at the time
Jehu met her in Jezreel).

Do you see evidence of the spirit of Jezebel in your
Church? To many Christians today who hold the doctrine of Jezebel, Christianity is a matter of the heart only;
one's physical appearance is immaterial. Most modern
Christians who try to maintain moral standards in dressing would dress fairly decently to attend Church but
dress poorly when going to a shopping mall, for example. This dichotomy of life is not what we have learned
of Christ. Whoever is in Christ is a New Creation, a city
built on a hill, a lighted lamp; the salt of the earth. This
light must shine everywhere we go; we cannot have one
image in the Church and another out there in the world.

Many Churches have degraded to the extent that
there is no longer any demarcation between the "believer" and the unbeliever. The two would look the same in
many ways. Our outward appearance is an expression
of the fullness of our hearts. Our hearts usually dress
before our bodies do. Dressing has a message; a motive.
Moral decay in a Church, quite often, translates to sen-

sual dressings and makeup; the end result of which is idolatry, lust and sexual immorality in various forms. I agree that dressing has a cultural component to it. However, in every culture around the world, there are standards (not necessarily written down somewhere) of good dressing. Sadly here in the United States, standards of morality have fallen so low and the society is so culturally heterogeneous that it is hard to define boundaries of what is meant by decent dressing. Much of what is accepted today as acceptable dressing, especially for women, was a taboo about a century ago.

Some of the things introduced by this spiritual queen, Jezebel, have become "untouchables" in the lives of those affected. An idol is anything in our lives that we won't let anyone touch carelessly. If we have things in our lives other than the Lord Jesus Christ, which if touched, would lead us to react like a caterpillar or a snake that has been struck, those would be problem areas or idols. I went to a Church meeting and found a lady very poorly dressed who led worship. Thereafter, I approached this lady privately, thanked her for her ministration and tried encouraging her to dress better in the future. You can guess how that went. She was offended and told me rudely that each time she dressed, it was to please herself and that she cared little about what anyone else thought about her. Well, this response showed that the things she had on were "untouchables". The Bible says we must consider one another, especially those weak in the faith. If food causes my brother to be offended, I would give up meat, lest I should cause my brother to stumble. Some Christians today do not care about the impact of their lives on those around them. A true believer in Christ lives in the consciousness of being the salt of the earth or a lighted candle, meant to light up his/her community, leading the people to the Lord.

Although the above focused mostly on women, men are not exempt from the spirit of Jezebel. In **3 John 1:9**, we read

> *"I wrote unto the church: but Diotrephes, who loveth to have the preeminence among them, receiveth us not".*

Diotrephes was an arrogant brother in this Church, who loved to always be in charge. This is reminiscent of the spirit of Jezebel; this spirit is very bossy. Jesus promises Churches with this spirit judgment and death unless they repent.

THE CHURCH IN SARDIS

"And unto the angel of the church in Sardis write; These things saith He that hath the seven spirits of God, and the seven stars; I know thy works, that thou hast a name that thou livest, and art dead. Be watchful, and strengthen the things which remain, that are ready to die: for I have not found thy works perfect before God. Remember therefore how thou hast received and heard, and hold fast, and repent. If therefore thou shalt not watch, I will come on thee as a thief, and thou shalt not know what hour I will come upon thee. Thou hast a few names even in Sardis, which have not defiled their garments; and they shall walk with me in white: for they are worthy. He that overcometh, the same shall be clothed in white raiment; and I will not blot out his name out of the book of life, but I will confess his name before my Father, and before His angels. He that hath an ear, let him hear what the Spirit saith unto the churches" (**Rev. 3:1-6**).

The Church in Sardis represents churches which are spiritually dead but have a great reputation or name of being alive. However, such Churches simply go through empty religious motions which are actually lifeless. Many people esteem such churches. They have a **"name"** for being alive but are simply busy, yet guilty. This **"name"** or fame could result from their past exploits (may be the Lord once moved in such Churches before in a tremendous way or may be, the founders were especially anointed but when they died, the ministries died with them). Fame could also come from fabulous infrastructure and other establishments like schools and hospitals. Another source of fame could be wonderful philanthropic activities around the world. All such things which may give a **"name"** to a Church do not necessarily mean that the Church is alive. Many Churches are busy Many churches are busy (with many activities which entertain the flesh) but are spiritually dead but are spiritually dead.

The rebuke from the Lord shows indeed that when the He looks at our lives and His Church, He desires to see life. God always seeks life and good fruit from His Vineyard, the Church. Unfortunately, some have lost the true life in the Spirit. Rather than cry out, some prefer to cover up with religious activities.

Churches fitting the frame of Sardis have a few things remaining. Their works are not perfect in the sight of God. This implies the Lord seeks perfection. Jesus said *"Be ye therefore perfect, even as your Father which is in heaven is perfect"* (**Matthew 5:48**). Paul likewise said *"…let us go on unto perfection…"* (**Hebrews 6:1**). Although we may always see imperfections in our lives, we must daily strive to be ever closer to the Lord. This is the striving which was in the Apostle Paul when he mentioned pressing on daily towards the mark of the high calling

in Christ. Sardis Churches are dead and lack this striving for perfection. Their works are not perfect before the
Lord. However, they are blinded by their fame or name
for being alive.

The Lord urges such Churches to arise and strength-
en the things which remain and are ready to die. This
suggests that spiritual dead is a process (sometimes,
a long one). This is true of our individual lives and of
the Church. Spiritual things die in us gradually, one
at a time. You may first lose your quiet time with the
Lord; then lose your Bible meditation; then your ability
to witness; then before you know it, you are telling lies
or exaggerating and so on. It's always a process. So for
Sardis Churches, many (but not all) things are dead, and
the things remaining are ready to die. Oh, how true this
is of many of our Churches which once were filled with
the fire of God's Holy Spirit. The anointing has departed from some of those Churches along with convicting
messages. However, one could still find a few things like
good music which remain but are dying, in the sense
that the music is becoming more and more corrupted
or worldly.

Nevertheless, God will always have a remnant that
has not soiled their garments. Sardis Churches have a
remnant that has not bowed the knee to spiritual corruption. While He urges compromisers to arise, repent
and strengthen the things which remain, He promises
a close walk with those who have kept the faith. This
shows that without repentance, no one can have access to God as to walk with Him. Only those who upon
receiving salvation from God, keep their garments by
practical righteousness can walk with God. Sadly, this
number is always few. The Lord says He has a few people in Sardis Churches who are on the narrow path to
life. These would walk with Him in white, for they are

worthy; having renounced all filthiness of the flesh and of the spirit.

THE CHURCH IN PHILADELPHIA

"And to the angel of the church in Philadelphia write; These things saith he that is holy, he that is true, he that hath the key of David, he that openeth, and no man shutteth; and shutteth, and no man openeth; I know thy works: behold, I have set before thee an open door, and no man can shut it: for thou hast a little strength, and hast kept my word, and hast not denied my name. Behold, I will make them of the synagogue of Satan, which say they are Jews, and are not, but do lie; behold, I will make them to come and worship before thy feet, and to know that I have loved thee. Because thou hast kept the word of my patience, I also will keep thee from the hour of temptation, which shall come upon all the world, to try them that dwell upon the earth. Behold, I come quickly: hold that fast which thou hast, that no man take thy crown. Him that overcometh will I make a pillar in the temple of my God, and he shall go no more out: and I will write upon him the name of my God, and the name of the city of my God, which is new Jerusalem, which cometh down out of heaven from my God: and I will write upon him my new name. He that hath an ear, let him hear what the Spirit saith unto the churches. (**Rev. 3:7-13**).

The noun "Philadelphia" derives from two Greek words: "philos" meaning "loving", and "adelphos" meaning "brother". Therefore, Philadelphia means "brotherly love". Churches fitting this frame have members who truly love each other and who love the Lord and His truth. Those members have kept the Word of God's patience. What does Jesus mean by *"the word of my patience"*? This suggests that these disciples remained faithful to God, clinging to His Truth even in the most difficult times. These disciples distanced themselves from liars; false Jews who were of the synagogue of Satan. Yes, there is such a thing as *"the synagogue of Satan"*. This is usually not a meeting place for witches, wiccas and wizards, per se. Rather, a synagogue of Satan is quite often a Church whose doctrinal teachings exalt the principles of Satan's kingdom as opposed to the Kingdom of God. Whereas Churches exist today with the name "Church of Satan", these are not the kind Jesus referred to as "the synagogue of Satan". The members of the synagogue of Satan claimed to be Jews worshipping God in truth, but were liars. This is unlike members of the Church of Satan today who out rightly identify with the worship of Satan. Therefore the synagogue of Satan represents Churches purportedly serving our Lord Jesus Christ, but which indeed worship Satan. Some Churches today are governed entirely by worldly principles. Such are synagogues of Satan.

The Lord promised to humble all such hypocrites before His faithful disciples. Our God usually makes a difference between the just and the unjust. With the pure, God shows Himself pure; but with the froward, He behaves frowardly. Therefore, He humiliates hypocrites but exalts those who keep the Word of His patience, and shows to others how much these faithful ones have loved Him. He boasted of Job to Satan. God has a tendency of bragging about His faithful ones who keep the Word of His patience.

Philadelphian Churches consist of members with a little strength. This speaks of their meekness and humility. Yes, we must see this phrase positively, rather than negatively. Our Lord Jesus Christ is described as "*...a tender plant, and as a root out of a dry ground...*" (**Isaiah 53:2**), referring to His humility and the difficult conditions He grew under while in the flesh. If the words "little strength" were negative, the Lord would have said something like "I have somewhat against you, that you have a little strength". But the Lord didn't say this. Rather, He said "thou hast a little strength, and hast kept my word, and hast not denied my name". We do not need much strength to stay faithful to the Lord. We only need a little strength. In fact, the more mature we get spiritually, the more we realize that we really need no strength at all; only a total surrender to the Lord. God's strength is perfected in our weakness. Those who claim to be strong will be fed with judgment.

> "*...but I will destroy the fat and the strong; I will feed them with judgment*" (**Ezekiel 34:16**).

The Lord resists the proud but gives grace to the humble. Philadelphian Christians trust only in God's merit; His saving strength. Therefore, the Lord fights for them, setting an open door before them which no one can close. He promised that if such continue in faithfulness, they would be kept from the hour of temptation. Our God is a preserver of His faithful ones.

We see that Philadelphia represents part of God's remnant in these perilous times. Jesus holds nothing against them. He rather promises to honor them. We see here that commendation before God is based on one's ability to keep the Word of His patience. This is a serious matter. Some in today's Churches have exchanged the truth of God's Word for a lie. Many are giving heed to seducing spirits, and the doctrines of devils; turning unto fables. Let us be the Philadelphian believers

"Holding forth the Word of life;..." (**Philippians 2:16**).

THE CHURCH IN LAODICEA

"And unto the angel of the church of the Laodiceans write; These things saith the Amen, the faithful and true witness, the beginning of the creation of God; I know thy works, that thou art neither cold nor hot: I would thou wert cold or hot. So then because thou art lukewarm, and neither cold nor hot, I will spue thee out of my mouth. Because thou sayest, I am rich, and increased with goods, and have need of nothing; and knowest not that thou art wretched, and miserable, and poor, and blind, and naked: I counsel thee to buy of me gold tried in the fire, that thou mayest be rich; and white raiment, that thou mayest be clothed, and that the shame of thy nakedness do not appear; and anoint thine eyes with eyesalve, that thou mayest see. As many as I love, I rebuke and chasten: be zealous therefore, and repent. Behold, I stand at the door, and knock: if any man hear my voice, and open the door, I will come in to him, and will sup with him, and he with me. To him that overcometh will I grant to sit with me in my throne, even as I also overcame, and am set down with my Father in his throne. He that hath an ear, let him hear what the Spirit saith unto the churches" (**Rev.3:14-22**).

Laodicea represents Churches which are materially and financially rich but spiritually destitute. The above description fits most western Churches which are so cold, so dead. Yet, those Churches are wealthy and their staff are well salaried. The Lord despises their physical wealth. The things of this world are meaningless before God. Ours is a judged world which in its present state, is fading away. While in Jerusalem at one time, Jesus' disciples admired the Temple and spoke to Jesus of its beauty. Jesus responded by predicting its destruction (**Mark 13:1-2**). In this way, He despised what it looked like.

Laodicea was a commercial hub with plenty of wealth and business men. The Church was thus rich and their wealth turned their hearts away from God. They became lukewarm. There's nothing worse than being lukewarm. It is hard to describe what lukewarm is. It is a mixture of cold and heat (but in what percentages?). One thing God hates is "mixture". He doesn't want us to be a mixture of good and evil; light and darkness. Laodicean Christians are a mixture. They love Jesus but also love the world; they try to serve both God and mammon. Those who are a mixture benefit nothing from God; they forfeit His grace; and He spews them from His mouth. **Ezekiel 47:11** reads

"But the miry places thereof and the marishes thereof shall not be healed; they shall be given to salt".

There is a deep truth in this verse. The first 10 verses of **Ezekiel 47** describe a vision of living waters (the Holy Spirit) flowing from God's Temple in Jerusalem and bringing healing and fruitfulness wherever the water flew. Although these life-giving waters healed virtually anything on its path, we are told in verse 11 that the miry places and the marishes could not be healed. What a thing! "Miry places and marishes" are a mixture of soil and water; that is, mud. Swampy or muddy lands are not useful to farmers. Swampy or muddy lives are not useful to God too, except such lives are surrendered to be cleansed by Him. "Earth" speaks of human nature; our flesh – man was formed from earth. "Water" speaks of "the Holy Spirit"; or godliness in a sense. A person whose life is mud; a mixture of earth and water won't be healed by God's life-giving waters. All such lives are given over to salt. Jesus said *"Remember Lot's wife"* (**Luke 17:32**). Do you remember how she ended? She became a pillar of salt. Her life was a mixture. She tried to walk with God but also loved the world. When she left Sodom, all her treasures remained in Sodom; everything she had toiled and amassed over many years. God's Angel warned her and her husband to flee Sodom without looking back, as fire and brimstones rained from heaven upon Sodom and Gomorrah. However, since Lot's wife had her heart in Sodom where her treasure was, she couldn't help but look back to Sodom. Her heart yearned for material things even as she undertook the journey of faith with Lot. Her life was muddy and she became a pillar of salt. So does **Ezekiel 47:11** state that muddy places cannot be healed by the waters of the Holy Spirit but would become salt. Such salt is the kind that has lost its saltiness as our Lord put it; it is worthless and would be thrown away. Thus, the Lord promises to spew out the lukewarm Laodicean Christians.

Laodicea speaks of complacency and self-sufficiency. Churches fitting this frame are a complete mix of godliness and worldliness. One wouldn't find any difference between members of such Churches and the unsaved. Laodicean Christians pride themselves in their wealth. But the Lord describes them as wretched, miserable, poor, blind, and naked. Can you imagine how God views some of those you may think have a good life? Some of those living in mansions and driving expensive cars are indeed spiritually wretched, miserable,... However, the Lord shows His mercy and compassion by urging such to come to Him for transformation. Although He tells them "...*buy of me...*" He actually would offer freely all they need. This means that it doesn't matter how bad one's situation is spiritually. If we are ready to turn to God, He is always ready to cleanse, take away our blindness or ignorance, and cloth us. Therefore He tells all Laodicean Christians to be zealous and repent or turn to Him.

It is quite sad how our generation emphasizes materialism or money. Many modern Churches are simply money making enterprises. Most are filled with so called "prosperity preachers" who basically make merchandize of the people as the Bible put it. Such won't preach the Words of Christ

> "*For all these things do the nations of the world seek after: and your Father knoweth that ye have need of these things. But rather seek ye the kingdom of God; and all these things shall be added unto you*" (**Luke 12:30-31**).

OR those of the Apostle Paul

> "*If ye then be risen with Christ, seek those things which are above, where Christ sitteth on the right hand of God. Set your affection on things above, not on things on the earth*" (**Colossians 3:1-2**).

Laodicea is simply not a place for such messages. Jesus has completely been forced out of such Churches. The Lord of the Church now stands out and knocks. Do you notice that Christ was outside, seeking entry into the Laodicean Church? This is the case with every life or Church which is a mixture. God shares His glory with no one. Many Churches have welcomed the world into their midst and the Lord Jesus Christ has left such Churches too. However, His love for such people keeps Him at the door, knocking to see who is ready to repent and open his/her heart to Him.

CONCLUSION

The survey of the messages to the seven Churches of Asia minor was intended to shed further light on what the Church has lost. I belief these seven Churches are an allegory of today's global Church. We noticed that Jesus called each Church He rebuked to repentance as a key to restoration. God is a merciful God. No matter how much we are fallen, there is always hope. The Lord accepts and transforms any sinner who returns to Him in deep contrition or penitence. Be zealous, therefore, and repent as you meditate on your own personal life to determine what you have loft or forfeited in Christ. We will now move on to discuss the significance of **"why the loss?"** and **"where it was lost?"** These specific questions are critical in our pursuit of restoration. You see, in the Parable of the lost coin (**Luke 15:8-10**), the owner concentrated on sweeping her own house, not any other house. This was because she knew where the coin had been lost. If she left her house and went sweeping a million other houses, she would never find the missing coin because it simply won't be in any of those houses. There are people who lose things but seek them in the wrong places.

PART II

WHY AND WHERE?

Four questions are important to a people who have determined to settle scores with God and their enemies and guarantee full and permanent restoration. These are:

- What was lost?
- Why was it lost?
- Where was it lost?
- How shall it be recovered and permanently kept?

Part I of this book dealt with the first question. The devastating work of Satan on the Church and our individual lives was discussed in the first three Chapters to reveal what the Church has lost. First, we analyzed the work of the palmerworm, locusts, cankerworm, and caterpillars. Then we discussed the loss of the walls and gates of the Daughter of Zion. Next we examined the messages of our Lord Jesus Christ to the seven Churches in Asia Minor. All of these helped reveal what we should be crying for as we press for revival and restoration. As mentioned previously, no one can cry properly for restoration without first knowing what has been lost.

Having determined what was lost, the next key issue is the question of why it was lost. Without understanding *why*, one can't address the right issues that should lead to restoration or they may recover what was lost but lose it again. Addressing the question of *why* leads to another important question of *where*. Defining *where* enables one to arrive at an honest assessment of the extent of spiritual decay. These two questions will be addressed here in **Part II**.

CHAPTER FOUR

WHY THE LOSS?

The first thing to note is that God never plans to take back the blessings He gives to the Church or to us. It is not His will that we rise today, fall tomorrow, rise the next day, and so on. The Bible says"

> *"But the path of the just is as the shining light that shineth more and more unto the perfect day"* (**Proverbs 4:18**). *"They go from strength to strength, every one of them in Zion appeareth before God"* (**Psalms 84:7**).

The Bible does not say, "The path of the just shines today, gets dark tomorrow..." Your path is supposed to shine more and more. According to God, we should grow from strength to strength; that is, we should continuously grow. Every blessing we receive from God is a seed that is expected to grow continuously and lead us to true greatness before Him. This is why the Lord Jesus Christ likens the Kingdom of God to a mustard seed that when sown is the least. But when it grows, it is the largest of all trees (**Mark 4:30-32**). Likewise, in the Parable of the Talents, we see that God expected all the talents to grow and multiply. The slothful servant who failed to multiply His talent was condemned (**Matthew 25:14-30**). What usually scares me the most in this latter parable is the fact that the servant who buried his talent was judged and condemned. He returned the talent to his master but still was condemned. What then would happen to those servants who lost their talents entirely? I am reminded of one of the sons of the prophets who borrowed an axe head and went to cut wood with the Prophet Elisha. This account is in **2 Kings 6:1-7**. You should notice how hard this young prophet cried when the borrowed axe head fell into the Jordan River. He knew it was borrowed and that he couldn't afford a replacement (more on this in the next chapter). We too must not take lightly this matter of seeking to reclaim spiritual treasures we have lost over the years.

When God brought the children of Israel into Canaan, He intended to plant them there permanently.

"Thou hast brought a vine out of Egypt: thou hast cast out the heathen, and planted it" (**Psalms 80:8**).

It was never God's will to later strengthen Nebuchadnezzar in order to wreak havoc in the land of Israel and carry away people and treasures from the Temple in Jerusalem. Although God, in His mercy, makes provision for repentance and restoration, it is never His wish to see His people backslide or lose the blessings He bestows upon them. This is why after Israeli captivity, God again promised to plant them in their own land so firmly that no enemy could uproot them.

"And I will plant them upon their land, and they shall no more be pulled up out of their land which I have given them, saith the LORD thy God" (**Amos 9:15**).

God's covenant with those He calls to be His people is the following

"As for me, this is my covenant with them, saith the Lord; My Spirit that is upon thee, and my words

which I have put in thy mouth, shall not depart out of thy mouth, nor out of the mouth of thy seed, nor out of the mouth of thy seed's seed, saith the Lord, from henceforth and forever" (**Isaiah 59:21**).

We see, therefore, that God's desire for us is to abide permanently in His blessings or covenant. In **Romans 11:29,** we read: *"For the gifts and calling of God are without repentance."*

Although God's wish is for us to abide in His blessings permanently, sin has the potency of perforating our lives and causing Divine treasures to leak away. The Scriptures discussed above underscore the fact that we are to blame for any loss of spiritual territory for which we are to seek restoration. This is the starting point for anyone who cares about pursuing true restoration. To begin by pointing accusing fingers elsewhere is to strain out a gnat and swallow a camel. God can never be the cause of our loss; He is never tempted with evil. Evil comes upon us when our hearts are carried away by diverse lusts. Then we are enticed, sin, and bring a curse upon our lives. On God's part, He ever desires to bless us. However, by virtue of His holiness, we must suffer the consequences of our choices. God looks at the backslidden Church and weeps as He wept over rebellious Israel in these words:

"O that my people had hearkened unto me, and Israel had walked in my ways! I should soon have subdued their enemies, and turned my hand against their adversaries. The haters of the Lord should have submitted themselves unto Him: but their time should have endured forever. He should have fed them also with the finest of the wheat: and with honey out of the rock should I have satisfied thee" (**Psalms 81:13-16**).

The loss for which we need restoration is due to our failure to stay true to the Divine Covenant. It is always a result of **sins of omission** (that is, the good we failed to do) and **sins of commission** (that is, the evil we did). Throughout the Bible, we see that negligence or rebellion on the part of God's people has always been the reason for judgment. God is faithful to the faithful but pours His wrath on rebellious and compromising children. His wrath is always being revealed from heaven against all ungodliness and the unrighteousness of men who hold the truth captive in unrighteousness.

You remember the account about David and his soldiers in **1 Samuel 30**. These men went to assist the Philistines in battle, and upon returning the Amalekites had invaded the city and carried away all they owned, including their wives and children. When you read this story, you can immediately blame David and his men, who all left for battle, leaving no soldiers or watchmen to guard their city. Didn't they know that their enemies were around, waiting to take advantage of any carelessness or foolishness on their part? David and his men ought to know that they were at war and surrounded by enemies. They made a grave mistake. They were zealous for the ministry and left their homes uncovered and unguarded. See what the enemy did:

"And it came to pass, when David and his men were come to Ziklag on the third day, that the Amalekites had invaded the south, and Ziklag, and smitten Ziklag, and burnt it with fire; And had taken the women captive, that were therein: they slew not any, either great or small, but carried them away, and went on their way. So David and his men came to the city, and behold, it was burnt with fire; and their wives, and their sons, and their daughters, were taken

captive. Then David and the people that were with him lift up their voice and wept, until they had no more power to weep" (**1 Samuel 30:1-4**).

If you give a chance to the enemy (Satan), he will not spare anything that belongs to you. He will take away everything and leave you either wounded or burnt to ashes like Ziklag. What happened to David and his men has repeated itself in many lives and Churches because of this same error — **failure to watch!** The devil watches over his goods far better than we do. Jesus testified of this when He said:

"When a strong man armed keepeth his palace, his goods are in peace" (**Luke 11:21**).

Satan is an armed strong man who guards his own seriously and jealously. However, many Saints of God have forgotten that they have an adversary who is going around like a roaring lion, desiring to devour and seeking whoever is careless. This is why many righteous people have perished in their righteousness while the wicked have prolonged their days (**Ecclesiastes 7:15**). This is why many mighty men have fallen in battle as if they were not anointed with oil (**2 Samuel 1:21**). The number of moral scandals implicating "men of God" has increased in recent years, bringing reproach to the name of our God. Paul told the Romans: *"For the name of God is blasphemed among the Gentiles through you, as it is written"* (**Romans 2:24**). The devil has plundered many lives and Churches because of our failure to watch.

The reason? Our generation is plagued with many distractions. Satan, who is described as a thief and the Ancient Serpent who deceives the whole world, has introduced many deceptive distractions. When I devoted time to edit this book and produce a second edition, Satan immediately put up a subtle fight. This fight varied from issues coming up in our local Church to which I needed to attend, to multiple "unnecessary" phone calls I received whenever I sat at the computer to work on the manuscript. I do not like ignoring peoples' calls (this is a weakness of mine). I would receive calls, some of which took forever to end because the individuals just kept talking and talking. Satan was behind all of these. He didn't want this book reprinted. He truly hates the content of this book (but I hope you don't hate it as well).

Today's modern society has many distractions, all of which are designed by our arch-enemy to keep us from focusing on God. Our generation is ignorant of the devices of the Devil. We claim to have knowledge, but it's only self-deception. While knowledge seems to be increasing, iniquity seems to be increasing. Our growth is in our ability to justify compromise; it's a negative growth. Some Churches have recently embraced practices that were unheard of (and deemed abominable) among God's people a century ago. For example, when I came to the Lord, divorce was taboo in the Church I attended. Today, believers are ready to go to Court and divorce freely. The waves of feminism, carnality, and immorality have taken a toll on several denominations, forcing them to adjust their doctrinal positions in order to accommodate the flesh.

Our generation has eaten sufficiently from the tree of the knowledge of good and evil, but has eaten little from the tree of life. Yes, when Jesus died on the cross, we (who are in Him) gained access to the tree of life. This is why Jesus said: "*And whosoever liveth and believeth in me shall never die. Believest thou this?*" (**John 11:26**). This declaration from our Lord suggests that the Angel who guarded the way to the tree of life (**Genesis 3:24**) ended his assignment once Christ died on the cross. The Son of Man came so that we may have life in abundance (**John 10:10**). He is the living bread from heaven, the water of life, and the light that lights everyone who comes into the world. How can it be that we serve such a God, and yet, many Churches and denominations are so dead and many in Zion are so oppressed?

One of the reasons is that those Churches lack devout watchmen stationed upon their walls; that is, in the place of continued travailing and watchful prayers. Some intercessors seem like soldiers who either do not fully know their duty or are entangled in civilian affairs, so to speak. Unfortunately, many lazy Saints rely on these inconsistent soldiers. The Lord told Jerusalem:

"I have set watchmen upon thy walls, O Jerusalem, which shall never hold their peace day nor night: ye that make mention of the Lord, keep not silence, And give him no rest, till he establish, and till he make Jerusalem a praise in the earth" (**Isaiah 62:6-7**).

God needs men and women who are given to prayer day and night. We are told to pray without ceasing. Prayer is necessary for our survival. The most important thing Jesus did while on earth was pray. Ministry was a secondary matter; it was the outcome of prayer. Today, however, tarrying before God in prayer is foreign to many Christians; we have become too busy to wait on the Lord. The neglect of watchfulness and consistent prayer is the primary reason for spiritual decay. Without these, the enemy easily comes in unhindered and sows his tares of worldliness, compromise, and so on. These grow and help bring our lives and Churches to *"Ichabod"* (a spiritual wilderness wherein the glory of God is departed).

Ours is a generation that places emphasis on periph-
eral issues and ignores weightier matters. For most of us
who plan Church-related events nowadays, the majority
of the time is spent deliberating on money, food, lodg-
ing, overall organization of event, and so on. Little attention is given to prayer. This is not the example Christ
gave us. The result is often worldliness in our events,
as we generally rely on the wisdom of this world, not
God's pattern.

Worldliness implies "seeking to do or be like the
world." For example, the Israelites were becoming
worldly when they demanded a king in order to be like
the heathen nations that surrounded them (**1 Samuel 8:4-9**). We have gone the way of the world in many
areas; we dress like the world, organize events like the
world, and have imported worldly bureaucracy into the
Church. These we do in order to avoid rejection, persecution, and/or appearing odd in a lost world. Fear
has led many to blend in and conform to the world. The
true disciples of Jesus, however, understand that they
are light and the world is darkness. Therefore, they keep
their distance from the world system.

> *"And we know that we are of God, and the whole
> world lieth in wickedness"* (**1 John 5:19**).

I am touched by this phrase *"the whole world."* This
suggests that there is nothing good in the world system (sounds like an overstatement?). Scripture says the
whole world lies in wickedness; that is, under the sway
of the wicked one (Satan). A true disciple of Christ understands this, and therefore, does not seek friendship
with the world. There is no common ground whatsoever between a true disciple of Jesus Christ and the world

system. The evil one succeeded to plant his tares only when men stopped watching and went to sleep.

> *"But while men slept, His enemy came and sowed tares among the wheat, and went his way"* (**Matthew 13:25**).

Truly, if we follow divine instructions to maintain the fire continually blazing on our altars, the enemy would have no means of sneaking in to steal, kill, or destroy.

> *"And the fire upon the altar shall be burning in it; it shall not be put out: and the priest shall burn wood on it every morning, and lay the burnt offering in order upon it; and he shall burn thereon the fat of the peace offerings. The fire shall ever be burning upon the altar; it shall never go out"* (**Leviticus 6:12-13**).

When God insists that the fire of prayer must never go out at our personal altars (note that the Temple in the Old Testament translates to our lives in the New Testament — **1 Corinthians 6:19**), it is because He knows better. God knows quite well what the enemy would do if the fire goes out. This is why He charges us to pray without ceasing. Jesus Christ understood this well and spent His years on earth praying with strong cries and tears. Consequently, He lost nothing in the days of His flesh except the son of perdition so that the scriptures might be fulfilled (**John 17:12**). Even when the enemy came desiring to snatch Peter, Jesus applied the same principle of prayer and Peter was preserved (**Luke 22:31-32**). The apostles learned this principle from their Master, and therefore, were able to sustain the revival in the early Church. They confessed:

"But we will give ourselves continually to prayer, and to the ministry of the word" (**Acts 6:4**).

They had learned from the Lord how to pray effectually and how to be fully given to prayer for fruitfulness in ministry. The spiritual treasures we receive from the Lord must be preserved by prayer. Without watchful prayer, our glory would gradually fade away. To be restored, we must then return to the place of deep contrition and persevering prayer.

Another reason for the loss for which we must now cry for restoration is the neglect of God's Word. Jesus told the Sadducees *"...Ye do err, not knowing the scriptures, nor the power of God"* (**Matthew 22:29**). A lack of knowledge of God's Word due to neglect results in us forfeiting many blessings. God's Word is the source of true faith that leads us to obtaining promises in Him. Again, when we fail to continue in prayer, the locusts attack God's Word in our lives, causing spiritual poverty and erroneous practices. The Lord's counsel to each of us is the following:

"This book of the law shall not depart out of thy mouth; but thou shalt meditate therein day and night, that thou mayest observe to do according to all that is written therein: for then thou shalt make thy way prosperous, and then thou shalt have good success" (**Joshua 1:8**).

Notice here that God didn't command Joshua to go learn His Word from the Priests or Prophets in Israel. God charged Joshua to study and meditate on His Word. This is the only way to grow properly in the Lord. Many Christians are being deceived easily today because they have no time for the Lord; they are unable to spend time before God to study and meditate on His Word daily. When you don't meditate on God's Word, it's hard to discern His voice or His will. It would also be easy to fall prey to deceiving spirits and the doctrines of demons. The Berean Christians were given to routine Bible meditation. Hence, they studied their Bibles daily to confirm Paul's teachings (**Acts 17:11**). The Bible describes them as noble. There is nobility associated with the routine practice of studying and meditating on God's Word.

Our generation is permeated with much deception. The Apostle John, during his own time, mentioned that many false prophets were already in the world (**1 John 2:18**). Therefore, in our time, it is safe to state that there are multitudes of false prophets, teachers, apostles, pastors, or evangelists in the world.

Many truths of God's Word have been adulterated or replaced; new teachings and Bible translations have emerged. Some of these modern Bible translations either modify specific verses to suit the purposes of the translators, eliminate whole verses, or cut verses short. For example, the King James Version (KJV) of the Bible renders **Romans 8:1** as: *"There is therefore now no condemnation to them which are in Christ Jesus, who walk not after the flesh, but after the Spirit."*

The New International Version (NIV) renders the same verse as: *"Therefore, there is now no condemnation for those who are in Christ Jesus."* Notice that the NIV rendering of this Scripture is quite misleading, suggesting that once a person is in Christ, he or she cannot be condemned. This supports the erroneous doctrine of eternal security of salvation in Christ. The KJV rendering of **Romans 8:1** shows that lack of condemnation is only for those Christians who constantly follow the leading of the Holy Spirit, as opposed to their flesh. We know that against the workings of the Holy Spirit, there is no law (**Galatians 5:23**). These subtle schemes of Satan (in altering Scriptural truths) are not noticeable to superficial Christians who have no time to sit at Jesus' feet to be taught the truths of the Kingdom of Heaven.

Insufficient or misguided prayers and the lack of Bible meditation are the prime causes of spiritual loss or decay. We can enumerate multiple sins of omission and commission that have sealed our heavens and led to this present spiritual wilderness. However, these are but the result of the neglect of prayer and the pure Word of God. The Apostles of Christ gave themselves wholly to these two things, but most of us haven't.

There is something in physics called *principle*. To physicists, a *principle* is a guiding role on how things work in a specific area of life. An example is the *principle of energy conservation,* which suggests that the overall energy of any isolated system is fixed no matter what changes it undergoes. God's Kingdom also has principles. For example, God says, *"And ye shall seek me, and find me, when ye shall search for me with all your heart"* (**Jeremiah 29:13**). This is a principle that says God rewards seekers who look for Him with their whole heart. God is a rewarder of those who diligently seek Him (**Hebrews 11:6**). This implies that those who seek God without diligence have little reward, and those who do not seek Him at all have zero reward. This principle cannot be violated. God rewards those who seek Him diligently. You will notice that when Jesus was on earth, He sought the Father diligently every day. That was because He understood that the principles of God's Kingdom cannot be violated. When God desired to save backslidden Israel, He sought a faithful person among them who could stand before Him to intercede. Finding none, He destroyed the people and the land (**Ezekiel 22:29-31**).

Without prayer, God could not save a judgment-deserving nation. This is because His Kingdom principle on prayer cannot be violated and people still somehow get blessed. We cannot live prayerless lives and still expect God to be with and bless us.

Another principle of God's Kingdom says, "*For where your treasure is, there will your heart be also*" (**Luke 12:34**). This principle can also not be violated. It is not possible for one to have his or her treasure here on earth, and yet, set his or her heart on things in heaven as mentioned in **Colossians 3:1-3**. A person's heart will always be where his or her treasure is. When we neglect divine principles that govern the Kingdom of God and substitute these with worldly wisdom and methodology, we lose or forfeit the treasures which are ours in the Lord. This is the reason for our loss and need for restoration.

Finally, **preaching and teaching are not our primary needs in these last days (as a Pastor, I'm not downplaying these). For restoration to occur, we must learn to weep in the place of prayer; we need to shed tears and pour out our souls before the Lord. This is what brought revival at different points throughout Church history. Our generation is filled with knowledge and technology, but there are few who tarry before the Lord daily, pleading with tears for their lives, families, Churches, and communities.**

We have had many wonderful seminars, conferences, Church growth events, and so on with nice displays on our pulpits. Yet, little has come out of most of these activities, and we seem to either maintain a spiritual status quo or are backslidden. We need to do more than organize events; we need to travail before the Lord. We need to come out of empty religious routines that take us nowhere with the Lord.

CHAPTER FIVE

WHERE WAS IT LOST?

The question of *where* our treasures or graces were lost is critical to restoration. As I mentioned before, without ratifying this matter of "*where*," our prayer will be arbitrary. We need to know *what* we lost, as well as *why* and *where* it was lost. We dealt with the question of "*what*" in the first part of this book; then we tackled the question of "*why*" in the previous chapter. Here, we shall dwell on the question of "*where*."

To approach this question, let us begin with the account in **2 Kings 6** concerning Elisha and the sons of the prophets.

> "*And the sons of the prophets said unto Elisha, Behold now, the place where we dwell with thee is too strait for us. Let us go, we pray thee, unto Jordan, and take thence every man a beam, and let us make us a place there, where we may dwell. And he answered, Go ye. And one said, Be content, I pray thee, and go with thy servants. And he answered, I will go. So he went with them. And when they came to Jordan, they cut down wood. But as one was felling a beam, the axe head fell into the water: and he cried, and said, Alas, master, for it was borrowed. And the man of God said, **Where fell it?** And he shewed him the place. And he cut down a stick and cast it in thither; and the iron did swim. Therefore said he, Take it up to thee. And he put out his hand, and took it*" (**2 Kings 6:1-7**).

In the above passage, we find that the sons of the prophets went to cut trees in order to build a dwelling place. In the course of felling the beams, the axe head of one of them fell into the Jordan. This man did two good things immediately following his loss. First, he cried out **immediately**. Second, he cried to a man who could actually help him or who had the answer to his problem. These two things are important for the recovery of what we have lost. We need to cry out immediately when we sense a loss in our lives. The young man cried to Elisha; we are to cry to the Lord, not to contemporaries who themselves need help. Imagine that this young prophet did not cry immediately. What would have happened if he had postponed his cry to some ideal time in the future? The swift waters of the Jordan River would have swept away the axe head, complicating chances of recovery.

We ought to cry out as soon as we realize we've lost something precious. The woman in the Parable of the lost coin cried out and went searching as soon as her coin was lost. The shepherd in the Parable of the lost sheep, likewise, went searching as soon as his sheep went missing. The young prophet screamed immediately and spontaneously saying, *"Alas Master, for it was borrowed."*

You see, if it wasn't borrowed, he could keep quiet and ignore the loss. But now, he had to face the owner of that axe head upon returning. Our entire lives are borrowed from the Lord. The earth is the Lord's and the fullness thereof. You and I actually own nothing, not even our very lives. God created all things for His pleasure, including you. He borrowed us His breathe of life. This is why we will be required to render account to Him on the last day. It is because we are mere stewards, and it is required of stewards to render account from time to time.

The matter of crying immediately is important. First, it shows that the person crying values what has been lost. Second, the "person" who took away that treasure is not far gone and can be easily apprehended. It is not only Satan who steals from our lives and Churches. God too takes away the candle stick from those who choose the path of compromise (**Revelation 2:5**).

"Seek ye the Lord while he may be found, call ye upon him while he is near: Let the wicked forsake his way, and the unrighteous man his thoughts: and let him return unto the Lord, and he will have mercy upon him; and to our God, for he will abundantly pardon" (**Isaiah 55:6-7**).

We are exhorted here to call upon the Lord while He is near. What a thing! It means God is not near always. If a man forsakes God's ways and God takes away the candle stick from him, God is not always going to be near. I know you are asking, "how about God's grace? Does it not make provision for all things?" Yes, we can always return to God anytime in repentance and be restored. If we return, the Lord will always bring us again to our original state (or better); He is the God of restoration and always turns again to those who turn to Him in repentance.

"Therefore thus saith the LORD, If thou return, then will I bring thee again, and thou shalt stand before me: and if thou take forth the precious from the vile, thou shalt be as my mouth: let them return unto thee; but return not thou unto them" (**Jeremiah 15:19**). *""Therefore say to them, 'Thus says the LORD of hosts, "Return to Me," declares the LORD of hosts, "that I may return to you," says the LORD of hosts"* (**Zechariah 1:3**).

However, some are unable to truly return after taking far too long to cry out for God's help. Esau found no place of repentance, although he sought it carefully with tears (**Hebrews 12:17**). Scriptures say it is impossible to renew some to repentance after they have known the grace of God but chosen to abuse it (**Hebrews 6:6**).

I remember one of my Pastors giving us a testimony about a friend he once had. When this friend was born, only one of his testicles had descended into the scrotal sack. Later in life after having received the Lord, he went to visit his brother, who was married at the time. His brother's wife (that is, his sister-in-law) knew about his condition and used this to mock him. On one fateful day, the two got into a quarrel and his sister-in-law mocked him saying, *"Are you a man with only one testicle?"* It turned out that she did this in the presence of one other girl. Satan uses mockery as one of his weapons for attempting to get people out of faith in Christ. This man felt truly humiliated by his sister-in-law. In order to prove his manhood, he decided to have sex with the girl who had overheard. After this incident, this man completely backslid and went back into the world. Years later, my pastor found this friend and attempted witnessing Christ to him. He asked him, *"John (not his real name), when are you coming back to the Lord?"* His friend got so angry at this question and asked him to leave his presence immediately. This story shows how it's possible for someone to leave the faith for good.

God's grace has an elastic limit. Although God forgives any sinner who returns to Him in repentance, not all return. Some have past feeling (**Ephesians 4:19**) and won't even feel when the Lord chastens them. Their hearts are hardened or obstinate and returning is impossible. Some of the Churches that are completely dead today were once alive and filled with God's Spirit. Prolonged compromise brought those Churches to where they are today.

> *"O LORD, are not thine eyes upon the truth? thou hast stricken them, but they have not grieved; thou hast consumed them, but they have refused to receive correction: they have made their faces harder than a rock; they have refused to return"* (**Jeremiah 5:3**).

Some return, but not to the Lord.

> **"They return, but not to the most High**: *they are like a deceitful bow: their princes shall fall by the sword for the rage of their tongue: this shall be their derision in the land of Egypt"* (**Hosea 7:16**).

What a thing! How can it be that a person who back-slides can decide to return but does not return to the Lord? The question then is: "what do such backslidden Christians return to?" Do they return to religion? They likely return to religious forms that may be new to them. However, they do not return to the Lord of true restoration. If you are reading this and the Holy Spirit opens your eyes to return, do well to return to the Lord, not to some empty religious routine. Come to Him, as He alone can change our lives (**Jeremiah 4:1**). What else can people return to instead of the Lord? People can return half-heartedly. They turn to the Lord but not with their whole hearts; they do it feignedly. In this way, the Lord still sees such as not having returned to Him.

> *"And yet for all this her treacherous sister Judah hath not turned unto me with her whole heart, but feignedly, saith the Lord"* (**Jeremiah 3:10**).

The above was intended to shed further light on the importance of returning to cry out to God immediately or as soon as we sense a spiritual loss in our lives or Churches. We now return to the key text for this Chapter (that is, **2 Kings 6:1-7**). When the young prophet cried out, Elisha immediately asked him *"where fell it?"* As far as God is concerned, precision is important. You have to bend down in prayers to find out **where** and **why** you lost the things you lost. These two questions of *why* and *where* are very much interconnected. Without determining *why*, it is hard to ascertain *where*. If we seek God sincerely, He will show us *why* our lives or ministries are the way they are. God can show you great and negative things in your life that you didn't know of if you start calling on Him. Therefore, we each need to dig until we uncover our foundations and discover secrets that have long been buried, possibly for years. You know, sin is only dealt with when squarely faced. This is the only way out. One cannot cover his or her sin for 30 years and expect it to die. Not at all. Even after 50 years, all it can do is to find him or her out.

> *"...be sure your sin will find you out"* (**Numbers 32:23**).

There are folks who try to avoid or who pretend not to know their transgressions. Quite often, people know their sins. When the storm hit the Prophet Jonah at sea with other travelers, Jonah knew immediately that it was because of his rebellion against God. The children of Israel confessed that they knew their iniquities.

> *"For our transgressions are multiplied before thee, and our sins testify against us: for our transgressions*

*are with us; and **as for our iniquities, we know them**"* (**Isaiah 59:12**).

Some would pray, saying "Oh Lord, I don't know why my life or ministry is rotten like this." But is it true that they really do not know why? As I mentioned before, sincerity in prayer is what leads us to the full revelation of *why* the mess and *where* it occurred or began. This is the starting point for seeking restoration. It is unwise to begin by praying arbitrarily and confessing "unknown sins" with such words as "Oh Lord, if I have sinned against you, forgive me." When you are serious about restoration, you do not pray with "if." You seek the right knowledge of your condition or life and call things by name in your prayers. Without this, all else you do will be as good as sowing among thorns: a fruitless endeavor.

To illustrate the importance of knowing *where* we lost it, let us revisit our Lord's instruction to the Church in Ephesus.

*"Nevertheless I have somewhat against thee, because thou hast left thy first love. Remember therefore **from whence thou art fallen**, and repent, and do the first works; or else I will come unto thee quickly, and will remove thy candlestick out of his place, except thou repent"* (**Revelation 2:4-5**).

Restoration demands that we **go back** to do what we did before. This is the result of true repentance. In going back, however, we need to know the height from which we have fallen. This will help us muster the strength or impetus needed. This is why God instructs these Ephesian Christians to remember from *where* they had fallen so that in going back, they do not end somewhere in the middle but get to *where* they missed it. Details are necessary when it comes to the matter of restoration. We cannot handle things at the surface level. Summarizing will not help. We must go deep, to the beginning; we must mean real business with God. This is what it will take for you and me; it is what it will take for the Church to restore the lost glory. We must return to the beginning to do the things we did before. But suppose we do not know this beginning. How then shall we assess the extent of damage or loss? And how then shall we cry properly?

The sketch below will further clarify the issue of *where*.

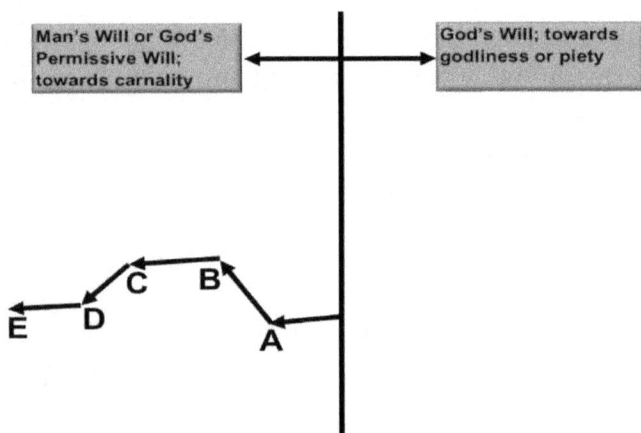

Figure 1. *Trajectory of the life of a Christian who rebels against God's Will at Point A and goes on to Points B, C, D, and E.*

This sketch depicts the life of a Christian who missed God's Will at point **A**. If a Christian rebels against God's Will and follows his or her own will (or the so-called permissive will of God), the rest of the steps that individual takes in life are wrong, as long as that person does not return to consider his or her ways and make right with God. If one sets out to resolve a mathematical problem and makes a mistake in the first step, even if the rest of the steps are correct, the final answer can never be right because the individual had a foundational problem. When the Psalmist asks: *"If the foundations be destroyed, what can the righteous do?"* (**Psalms 11:3**), it is because once the foundation has a problem, every other effort is in vain. Imagine Prophet Jonah, who fled from God's Will. If he had successfully reached Tarshish to begin a ministry, would God approve that ministry? Suppose he did this and went on pastoring for 30 years and enjoying the good life of Tarshish. Would 30 years of ministry annihilate the foundational problem of his life, one of rebellion against God's will? I think not. When Jonah turned away from God's Will, every other step he took in life was wrong up to the day he cried from the belly of the whale (**Jonah 2**).

> *"Woe unto him that buildeth his house by unrighteousness, and his chambers by wrong"* (**Jeremiah 22:13**).

If a foundation is unrighteousness, whatever stands on it is unrighteous. If the root is righteous, so too will the branches be (**Romans 11:16**). But if the root is defiled, the branches will also be unholy. I have seen Christians deliberately take wrong steps in life, trusting that the Lord will yet accept and bless them. I know God is quite merciful, but I won't deliberately sin because He is merciful. A Christian lady who lied to obtain a favor justified her lies by quoting Abraham who lied and was yet blessed by God. Never use a negative scenario in the Bible as justification for evil in your life. The fact that David committed adultery and got restored doesn't mean any of us should willfully indulge in sexual sin, counting on God's mercy.

After rebelling against God's Will (point **A**), the individual depicted in Figure 1 above moves on to points **B, C, D** and **E**. Whether these subsequent steps in the Christian's life are positive (e.g., beginning his or her own ministry, giving gifts, etc.) or negative (e.g., fraudulent acts, sexual immorality, etc.) is immaterial. As long as the individual does not return to address the foundational problem of rebellion against God, all else is rejected before God. This is why we are told:

> *"The sacrifice of the wicked is an abomination to the LORD: but the prayer of the upright is his delight"* (**Proverbs 15:8**). *"The sacrifice of the wicked is abomination: how much more, when he bringeth it with a wicked mind?"* (**Proverbs 21:27**).

Once a person rebels against God, his or her sacrifices are counted as an abomination to God. This sounds hard, but it's true. If God does not accept a person's life, He cannot accept the person's sacrifices or offerings. Suppose the said Christian now comes to his or her senses and wishes to seek restoration. If he or she returns from point **E** to point **B**, for example, instead of point **A**, can this person cry properly and address the real issues of his or her life? Certainly not. God demands that he or she goes back to point **A** where he or she first started going off, amends his or her ways, and begins to do the good he or she did before. This would be genuine repentance.

It must be noted, however, that there are certain errors that cannot be easily corrected. For example, Abraham getting a child through the slave girl, Hagar; Judah getting a set of twins through his own daughter-in-law, Tamar; and so on.

Such errors are difficult to correct, but those involved must repent deeply to be restored by the Lord. Getting married outside of God's Will for one's life is another example of such errors. A pastor once asked, *"The Bible says whatsoever God has joined together, let not man put asunder. Has every marriage been put together by God?"* Although it may be said that every marriage is not in God's Will, the Bible does not teach that a person can divorce his or her partner because they feel the spouse is not their rightful partner according to God's Will. If you married the wrong person, you should live with that person until death separates the two of you. I understand that due to the difficult times we live in, many Christians have become covenant breakers in this area of marriage. Our justification for divorce can never change the position of God, who says, *"I hate divorce; I hate putting away."* For errors that are difficult to correct, God in His sovereignty forgives the repentant individual and allows him or her to continue in His Will.

Finally, there can be no restoration without people going back to do the good they had forsaken. This has to be a deliberate action. One shouldn't have to wait for some special move of the Spirit before going back to seek restoration.

Moreover, crying immediately is important. Postponement may make it harder to trace one's path back to the beginning that God is asking him or her to return to. Therefore, learn to cry out immediately when something goes wrong with you. The day Tamar, David's daughter, was raped by her half-brother, Amnon, is the very day she cried out. In fact, she tore the garments of her virginity and put ashes on her head as soon as she was ejected from Amnon's house following the sexual assault (**2 Samuel 13**). Everyone in Israel who saw her knew immediately what had happened. Beloved, the day you stopped prophesying is the day you ought to cry out. The day you stopped evangelizing, praying, meditating on God's word, and so on, is the day you ought to cry out. If armed robbers break into your house and carry away everything and you hope to recover anything, you will not wait to cry out. You will do so immediately. Those of us in the USA will call 911 as soon as we possibly can. Did you dial the spiritual 911 on the day you sensed a backsliding in your life? Did you dial the spiritual 911 on the day you noticed your Church began to gradually die? There are things you lost, and instead of crying out, you developed other methods of going on in such a way that no one could detect that you had lost anything. There is plenty of cover up in Churches nowadays. There are people at the pulpits living in outright sexual immorality, and yet, doing ministry. They won't cry out. They would rather manage their decay than cry out for God's help. Do not be like one of these people.

PART III

COST AND EFFECTS OF RESTORATION

Having expounded on the critical issues of what the Church has lost, why, and where, we will now focus on what it will take to ensure full restoration, as well as on the effects of restoration. Any man who wants to build a house sits down and calculates the cost before setting out. Foolish people delve into many things in life without careful thought and waste a lot of energy without achieving anything tangible. Jesus took time again and again to explain the conditions for discipleship to all those who desired following Him. For example, He told a scribe who was anxious to follow Him the following:

> "...The foxes have holes, and the birds of the air have nests; but the Son of man hath not where to lay his head" (**Matthew 8:20**).

When it comes to walking with Jesus, we must each count the cost. This cost is rooted in our having to renounce the world and everything in it. It is rooted in our having to deny ourselves, bear our cross daily, and follow Him whole-heartedly with a willingness to suffer with Him if need be.

Spiritual backsliding is a consequence of Christians embracing things or practices that appeal to and gratify the lusts of their flesh, the lusts of their eyes, and the pride of their lives. To seek restoration is to choose to put away all of these and return to God in deep repentance. This could mean that a pastor chooses to return all the money he stole from the ministry he's been running; it could mean that a Christian returns all he or she obtained by theft; it could mean breaking off from evil relationships or alliances, and so on. Herein lies the cost of restoration.

Restoration has many wonderful consequences that cannot be all discussed in a single chapter of a book. Our Lord Jesus Christ came to the world to restore us back to our original state; that is, the state of being a people created in God's image and showing forth His glory and praises. Jesus came to bring us to the state Adam was in before his fall. This is why the ultimate purpose of our spiritual growth is our conformity to the image of Christ. In God's plan, He wants all of us in Christ to become of the same stock with Christ - Christlikeness. In this way, Christ would not be ashamed to call us His brethren (**Hebrews 2:11**). The effects of restoration discussed in this book are only a small portion of all that our God has prepared for us in Christ that eye has neither seen nor ear heard.

CHAPTER SIX

THE COST OF RESTORATION

The previous chapter touched on what it takes to ensure restoration. This chapter will discuss, in further detail, the cost of full and permanent restoration. As mentioned above, there is a cost associated with following Jesus. But this cost is not related to money. In summary, this cost has to do with your having to lay down your life for God. For restoration to be possible, there is a *"Human Responsibility"* and a *"Divine Responsibility."* Backsliding Churches and Christians must do their part and cooperate with God to do His part in bringing about true restoration.

THE HUMAN RESPONSIBILITY

(1.) GENUINE REPENTANCE

In the first chapter of this book, we discussed the work of the palmerworm, locusts, cankerworm, and caterpillars, and their spiritual implications. After the Lord used this metaphor to describe the spiritual state of backslidden Israel in the first chapter of the book of Joel, He immediately urged the Priests or ministers of the Altar to weep in repentance and to call on all Israel to do the same.

"Gird yourselves, and lament, ye priests: howl, ye ministers of the altar: come, lie all night in sackcloth, ye ministers of my God; for the meat offering and the drink offering is withholden from the house of your God. Sanctify ye a fast, call a solemn assembly, gather the elders and all the inhabitants of the land into the house of the Lord your God, and cry unto the Lord" **(Joel 1:13-14)**.

"Therefore also now, saith the Lord, turn ye even to me with all your heart, and with fasting, and with weeping, and with mourning: And rent your heart, and not your garments, and turn unto the Lord your God: for He is gracious and merciful, slow to anger, and of great kindness, and repenteth Him of the evil. Who knoweth if He will return and repent, and leave a blessing behind Him; even a meat offering and a drink offering unto the Lord your God? Blow the trumpet in Zion, sanctify a fast, call a solemn assembly: Gather the people, sanctify the congregation, assemble the elders, gather the children, and those that suck the breasts: let the bridegroom go forth of his chamber, and the bride out of her closet. Let the priests, the ministers of the Lord, weep between the porch and the altar, and let them say, Spare thy people, O Lord, and give not thine heritage to reproach, that the heathen should rule over them: wherefore should they say among the people, Where is their God?" **(Joel 2:12-17)**.

In the above, we find the human element in restoration. The first step to restoration is to admit that one has lost (or forfeited) God's blessings in one's life, ministry, or Church. Satan is a wise and subtle enemy. If someone broke into your home and stole away a big flat screen TV, you can easily replace that because the vacancy left by the theft would be quite obvious. Satan is wise and does not function like the thieves of this physical world. In spiritual terms, if Satan plans to steal "a TV" from your life, he also carefully plans on what He would replace the TV with in order to keep you busy and unconcerned with the loss. He may bring "a fake TV" to replace the original TV he takes away.

Satan works by way of substitution or replacement. He doesn't steal the same way mere mortals do. He always replaces the original with a counterfeit. In this way, those he steals from either do not notice the havoc he wreaks or are comfortable with their counterfeit. There are many Churches and individual Christians from whom Satan has stolen spiritual treasures (e.g., anointed music, anointed messages, godly fellowship, and so on). Satan has not left these lives and Churches vacant. He has simply replaced what they had with something fake (but perhaps more attractive and more alluring to the flesh). However, the unction of the Holy Spirit is gone from those lives or Churches, and the truth diluted.

Due to the subtle ways our enemy works, restoration tends not to be an obvious need to most Christians. Many have been blinded by the god of this world to their need of salvation or restoration. Some backslidden Christians simply cannot realize they have fallen so low. They measure themselves with other defeated soldiers in Zion who are at ease and who are pleasure lovers. I have met many Christians who justify compromise in their lives by citing backslidden men of God and their adulterated teachings. Of course, the backslider in heart is filled with his or her own ways. Such simply do not realize their true spiritual state. What a blessing, indeed, when the Lord helps open our eyes to the reality of our lives and ministries before Him. He did this to Isaiah, the Prophet, when He encountered him as we read in **Isaiah 6:1-8**. Admitting this true spiritual state (our fallen or backslidden state) is paramount and a necessary first step to seeking restoration. Without first admitting we have fallen, we can neither cry out in repentance nor seek true restoration. It wasn't until Isaiah saw his true nature that he cried out for God's help. It wasn't also until he cried out that God's Angel brought live coals from the Altar in heaven to burn his lips and purge his iniquity.

After admitting that we have fallen, the next step in seeking true restoration is to seek to know all that is lost (or forfeited) and why. Nehemiah was burdened for the restoration of Israel, especially the walls of Jerusalem. When he got to Israel, he did something quite revealing.

> *"So I came to Jerusalem, and was there three days. And I arose in the night, I and some few men with me; neither told I any man what my God had put in my heart to do at Jerusalem: neither was there any beast with me, save the beast that I rode upon. And I went out by night by the gate of the valley, even before the dragon well, and to the dung port, and viewed the walls of Jerusalem, which were broken down, and the gates thereof were consumed with fire. Then I went on to the gate of the fountain, and to the king's pool: but there was no place for the beast that was under me to pass. Then went I up in the night by the brook, and viewed the wall, and turned back, and entered by the gate of the valley, and so returned. And the rulers knew not whither I went, or what I did; neither had I as yet told it to the Jews, nor to the priests, nor to the nobles, nor to the rulers, nor to the rest that did the work. Then said I unto them, Ye see the distress that we are in, how Jerusalem lieth waste, and the gates thereof are burned with fire: come, and let us build up the wall of Jerusalem, that we be no more a reproach"* (**Nehemiah 2:11-17**).

There are lessons we should learn here. When you want to seek true restoration, you do not have to make it public news. If the Lord has touched you and revealed spiritual decay in your life or Church and is leading you to seek restoration, do not be quick to announce this. Those who talk too much about what they plan to do actually do little compared to those engaged in quiet labors. Real doers do not talk much.

When Nehemiah got to Jerusalem with the Divine Assignment of rebuilding Jerusalem's walls, he was there for three days, possibly praying. Thereafter, he arose by night to survey the land and acquaint himself with the extent of destruction. Without this acquaintance, he would be a poor preacher to the rulers of the land and the people. Likewise, our Lord Jesus Christ became a man of sorrows, acquainted with grief so that He may help them that grieve or are sorrowful; He was perfected by sufferings that He may become a true High Priest to us.

Nehemiah surveyed the land by night. You see, dear friend, important things happen by night. When a military plans attacks on critical enemy targets, they usually execute such plans by night. In **Isaiah 21:11** we read:

"The burden of Dumah. He calleth to me out of Seir, Watchman, what of the night? Watchman, what of the night?"

The watchman is expected to keep wake and watch by night. The situation of Dumah is deplorable, as their watchmen are seemingly asleep. They are not making good use of the night to change their situation. Then the Prophet cries, *"Watchman, what of the night? Watchman, what of the night?"* Night prayer is important. I am not saying you should only pray at night. Do not misunderstand the point here. But note that Jesus spent many nights praying on Mount Olives. He prayed in the Garden of Gethsemane by night prior to His arrest to be crucified. He prayed on Mount Olives all night before choosing His twelve apostles. Critical things happen by night.

So Nehemiah went by night to survey Jerusalem's walls in order to fully understand the extent of destruction. This is what we need to do spiritually. We must seek to understand the extent of spiritual decay in our own lives and Churches. If you are a recent believer in Christ, you probably do not understand what I am writing here. But let me tell you this: what you have met as "Church" since giving your life to Christ is not what God intended to be. If you want to understand what God's intention is for His Church, read the book of Acts and see how the Church used to be. Take note of how the glory of God was in the Church at that time. Compare with what we have today. That is how you understand that there has been spiritual decay that calls for a need for restoration.

Ezekiel, likewise, sought to be fully acquainted with the depth of backsliding among the Israelis he was commissioned by God to preach to. In **Ezekiel 2**, we find that the Lord commissioned Ezekiel and gave him the scroll to eat spiritually. After Ezekiel got to the Israelis in captivity, he said:

> "Then I came to them of the captivity at Telabib, that dwelt by the river of Chebar, and I sat where they sat, and remained there astonished among them seven days" (**Ezekiel 3:15**).

Seven is the number of completion. Ezekiel did not begin preaching as soon as he got to Telabib. He sat where the people sat for seven days, saying nothing. This is quite revealing. Unless you are acquainted with a situation, you do not have a mandate to speak to that situation. Unless we understand the extent of decay, we cannot truly cry the right cry for restoration. Ezekiel sought to acquaint himself completely with the situation. He was not just overwhelmed but pondered over the plight of the spiritually destitute Israelis. Do you find a correlation between what Ezekiel did here and what Nehemiah did by night? These two both sought to be fully acquainted with the situations for which they were sent to seek restoration.

Having understood and acquainted ourselves with decay or loss, we must then bend down in intense repentance to amend our ways and do the right things. As mentioned before, knowing how far we have gone into decay will enable us to build the right momentum before setting out on the race in pursuit of restoration. For example, if you see a bag of rice and think it is simply a pillow, you may send your left hand to pick it up, but you will not succeed. This does not mean you couldn't lift a bag of rice. It is just a problem of underestimation. Although God is the one who ultimately restores, the extent of prayer and how it is done is important. Remember, Jesus said, *"Howbeit this kind goeth not out but by prayer and fasting"* (**Matthew 17:21**). This means problems are of different magnitudes and require different magnitudes of prayer. We do not witness breakthroughs in certain things due to underestimation. We pray casually for serious issues that require intense, tearful prayers accompanied by fasting.

In **1 Samuel 1**, we read about the intense prayers of Hannah and how these birthed the baby Samuel. She had been praying casually year in and year out but remained barren. The year her prayers became *"the pouring out of her soul before the Lord,"* she became pregnant. We must learn to travail, literally. On the day she travailed in prayer, the High Priest accused Hannah of being drunk. You can imagine how she prayed that day. It must have been quite intense. Those are the kind of prayers we need for revival. Hannah's prayers were not just for a son. They were also meant to birth a new spiritual era in Israel that was in spiritual darkness at the time due to the ungodliness of Eli's sons serving as Priests. In a sense, Hannah was praying for revival; she wanted a son who would serve the Lord in a time when Israel was without a godly leader. The Lord granted her request; Samuel became a great Judge and Prophet whose word never fell to the ground.

Superficiality, fear and the love of pleasure are strong enemies of restoration. Restoration requires that we fully prepare our hearts to pay a sacrificial price, especially in prayer. Not knowing the extent of loss usually leads to underestimation of this price.

You see, the Prophet Elijah did not know the distance he had to cover and so he ate a little food and slept. But the angel advised him to eat more because his journey would be longer than he anticipated (**First Kings 19:5-8**). Likewise, when King David set out to pursue the Amalekites, all of his men took off with him. But some of them were ignorant of the cost of restoration, and so they fainted on the way, even though their wives, children, and property had also captured. They became so weary that they preferred to lose their wives and children forever.

> *"But David pursued, he and four hundred men: for two hundred abode behind, which were so faint that they could not go over the brook Besor"* (**1 Samuel 30:10**).

The men who fainted underestimated what it would take to get back their wives, children, and property. On the other hand, David and the other 400 men had resolved not to quit until they recovered everything. The

Lord had given them the assurance in this regard before they set out in pursuit of the enemy.

I am not talking here of our personal strength or effort. Certainly, without God, we can do nothing. I am talking about having the right determination, inner fortitude, and resolve to move with God in the race toward restoration. Only God by His grace and mercy can restore to us all we have lost. However, we must be fully resolved to run with God and see restoration come to fruition. In **Isaiah 62:6-7**, which I cited previously, we are told to give ourselves no rest and to give God no rest until He establishes and makes our lives (and Churches) a praise in the earth. A life or Church that becomes a praise in the earth is a life or Church that has been fully restored by the Lord. For this to happen, we must learn to give ourselves no rest, and to give God no rest.

Our Christian journey can be portrayed schematically as follows in Figure 2.

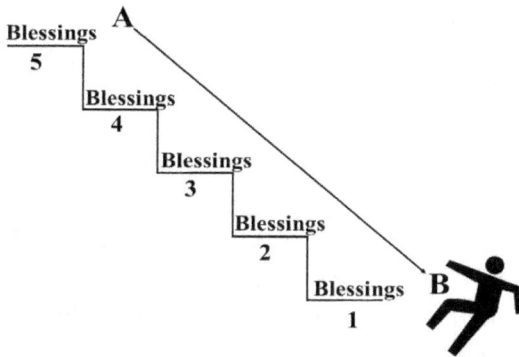

Figure 2. *Schematic of a Christian's journey from one level of spiritual experience to another (precept upon precept). The Christian falls spiritually from Level 5 (Point A) to Level 1 (Point B). Consequently, he or she loses the Blessings at Levels 2 to 5 and there is a need for Restoration.*

If a Christian falls from point **A** and rolls down to point **B**, he or she loses all the blessings at **levels 2** to **5** and would require more effort than initially used to climb back to point **A** and regain those blessings. The things we have lost were received from the Lord with little struggle. However, restoration is costly. It involves battling with unwilling enemies. It is easier to fall downward than to climb. It is easier to destroy than to build.

Although Figure 2 illustrates the life of a Christian who has fallen spiritually, the same is true of fallen Churches. According to the instructions given by the Lord through Prophet Joel, priests, ministers, and elders are called upon to be the ones to initiate restoration by raising a mighty cry in sackcloth and with fasting. The elders ought to understand the extent of decay more than any other person. Whereas spiritually younger folks may rejoice in mercy drops or crumbs, the spiritual elders in the Church, who had tasted the former wine or glory, ought to initiate a strong, earnest, and honest cry. Without raising an honest cry that's mindful of the true spiritual condition, the result could be partial restoration. **Ezra 3:11-12** reads:

> *"And they sung together by course in praising and giving thanks unto the Lord; because He is good, for His mercy endureth for ever towards Israel. And all the people shouted with a great shout, when they praised the Lord, because the foundation of the house of the Lord was laid. But many of the priests and Levites and chief of the fathers,* **who were ancient men that had seen the first house,** *when the foundation of this house was laid before their eyes, wept with a loud voice; and many shouted aloud for joy…"*

This was a situation of partial restoration wherein the rebuilt Temple in Jerusalem was of less glory compared to the one that had been destroyed. The chief of the fathers (the old men) who had seen the former house in its full splendor understood that the rebuilt house was inferior. Therefore, while young men celebrated, old men wept.

Today, while younger folks in the Church are celebrating apostasy, the old men, the chief of the Church fathers, ought to weep. The elders ought to blow the trumpet in Zion and cry out for restoration. Unfortunately, many leaders are blind and conquered by the world today such that they hardly will cry like the elders in the time of Israel's restoration. The Lord laments, *"Who is blind, but my servant? or deaf, as my messenger that I sent? who is blind as he that is perfect, and blind as the LORD'S servant?"* (**Isaiah 42:19**). The devil deceives such blind leaders into thinking that restoration is impossible or that God will just arise (without us doing anything) and restore all things before the end comes. Thus, you hear them speak of the old good days and regret the loss but do not cry. Others have lost hope of any possibility of restoration. If we need change, we must arise to action. Unfortunately, our generation is full of men and women who sit on the fence; they are experts at analyzing and criticizing Churches and other Christians but do nothing on seeking restoration. I have met Christians with a fastidious spirit, and I can tell you, many of those had no burden to travail before God for the restoration of their lives, families, and Churches. They were just experts at finger-pointing.

Since most pulpits are dead nowadays, you must not wait on your Church elders or Pastor to initiate restoration. As you read this book, and as the Lord witnesses in your heart, begin to cry out like Daniel (**Daniel 9**) and Nehemiah (**Nehemiah 1**). These men didn't wait on the elders or priests to initiate the cry in their own time. When the issue of restoration dawned on them, they began sobbing and groaning with fasting in secret without inviting anyone to join them. Nehemiah's mourning was so visible on his face that the king (Artaxerxes) could not be indifferent about it.

Many eyes do not open initially to the truth about the need for restoration. Pursuing restoration or revival usually begins with one man or a few people. If God challenges you through this book to pursue restoration, do not start by compelling other people immediately to join you. Apply the methods of Daniel or Nehemiah. The things written in the Bible are for our learning, and serve as an example for us. Spend some time to groan and weep in secret. This act is quite contagious. Before long, as you continue to groan in secret, your Church pulpit or other individuals around you will be affected. When that happens, you then have a few men to take along like Nehemiah (**Nehemiah 2:12**).

From there, proceed to include everyone. This is a method that always works. Note that when you start, there will be mockers and discouragers like Sanballat and Tobiah. These will come to you either as demons or physical beings telling you not to waste time on what will not yield fruits. They will suggest other "good" work for you to do rather than bend down for this crucial issue of restoration. They will threaten and try to intimidate you. Know that restoration is something the devil will fight against with all his might. Be as courageous and as determined as Nehemiah. Ask the same question he asked: "...*Should such a man as I flee?*" (**Nehemiah 6:11**). It takes the courage of David and Nehemiah to pursue restoration and not faint until we have overtaken our enemies and recovered all we lost.

Coming back to the book of Joel, we are counseled by the Lord to genuinely repent as the only remedy for our deteriorated lives. Throughout history, true repentance has hardly ever been without **fasting**. Fasting has far reaching effects. Take the case of Nineveh, where the people all repented deeply with fasting at the preaching of Jonah. Sucklings and animals fasted and God could not but turn their curse into a blessing. The Bible testifies:

> *"**And God saw their works,** that they turned from their evil way; and God repented of the evil, that He had said that He would do unto them; and He did it not"* (**Jonah 3:10**).

Yes, fasting is one of those good works that we are created in Christ to walk in. Whereas works do not lead us to salvation, faith without works is dead. Some people downplay the issue of fasting. However, if we must experience full restoration, it cannot be without fasting and lamentation. Our eyes have become dry. We need to cry like prophet Jeremiah, and the Lord will surely help us.

> *"O that my head were waters, and mine eyes a fountain of tears, that I might weep day and night for the slain of the daughter of my people"* (**Jeremiah 9:1**).

When Jeremiah desired tears, he ended up being known as the weeping prophet (see the Lamentations of Jeremiah). This means that the Lord does for us exactly what we ask Him to do in accordance with His will. Tears have far more power than all other words of supplication that we can use. God told Hezekiah:

"...I have seen thy tears..." (**Isaiah 38:5**).

Tears move God to action. The cry of the Israelites in Egypt made God restless, and He could not but arise to deal with their enemies and restore His people by sending Moses, whom he used mightily (See **Exodus 2:23-25**). Pray for tears. We need them today. The Lord didn't say through Joel, *"gather the elders and speak to the Lord."* Rather, he said, *"cry unto the Lord."* It has to be serious. It has to be deep and not superficial. It should go with restitution when necessary. You cannot steal someone's mobile phone, for example, and go to the secret crying for forgiveness from God (without refunding the phone) and expect an answer. I mentioned this previously. True restoration involves restitution. This should be done carefully, following the Lord's leading.

The Lord Jesus Christ did not teach us to wear sackcloth, as in the Old Testament, when fasting and mourning over our situation. Rather, He said:

> *"Moreover when ye fast, be not as the hypocrites, of a sad countenance: for they disfigure their faces, that they may appear unto men to fast. Verily I say unto you, They have their reward. But thou, when thou fastest, anoint thine head, and wash thy face; That thou appear not unto men to fast, but unto thy Father which is in secret: and thy Father which seeth in secret, shall reward thee openly"* (**Matthew 6:16-18**).

This is why I talked of weeping in secret. Don't blow a trumpet (or make a Facebook post, for example) when you are pursuing restoration. Do not place a post on Twitter to let your friends know you are seeking God in a new way. If you must blow a trumpet, well, do so only in Zion (that is, in your Church). Be as wise as Nehemiah. Rent your heart and not your garments. That is, your prayer should not be an outward display, but rather, an inner brokenness. It should involve the totality of your heart and spirit. Praying for restoration entails a complete turn to the Lord from our evil ways. It should eventually involve everybody (in the Church), exempting none. The issue of restoration is so serious that even honeymoon has no place.

> "...Let the bridegroom go forth of his chamber, and the bride out of her closet" (**Joel 2:16**).

In **Deuteronomy 24:5**, the Lord commanded that if a man in Israel was newly wed, he should neither go to war nor bear any other burdens. The person had to stay at home for one full year. Nevertheless, the matter of seeking restoration is quite serious; it is so serious that the bridegroom must go forth from his chamber and even the bride must leave her closet to fast and pray. Yes, beloved, when it comes to seeking restoration and revival, no one in the Church should be exempt. Restoration demands that we leave our "honeymoons," our places of comfort, to give ourselves to fasting and mourning.

(2.) REPAIR OF OUR ALTARS

After genuine repentance, our next responsibility is to repair our personal altars (the altar of the Lord) as Elijah did.

> "...And he repaired the altar of the Lord that was broken down. And Elijah took twelve stones, according to the number of the tribes of the sons of Jacob, unto whom the word of the Lord came, saying, Israel shall

be thy name: And with the stones he built an altar in
the name of the Lord: …" (**1 Kings 18:30-32**).

The altar of God is broken down through idolatry. Once the people of God start worshipping idols, God's altar automatically disintegrates. The reign of King Ahab was one of severe idol worship in Israel, and God's altar could not remain standing. Today, we have many idols in our lives and the Church. We worship the idols of television, Internet, food, sleep, leisure, clothes, money, and cosmetics, just to name a few. An idol is simply anything that has taken God's place in your heart or that retards your devotion and service to God. An idol can be a good thing, such as your career or spouse. Anything (good or bad) taking God's place in our hearts qualifies as an idol. This is why we are to hate all else, including our very lives, before we can truly walk with Jesus.

"…these men have set up their idols in their heart,
and put the stumbling block of their iniquity before
their face…" (**Ezekiel 14:3**).

If you are to experience full restoration, you must identify the idols in your life and arise like King Josiah to totally destroy and separate yourself from them.

"And Josiah was eight years old when he began to
reign, and he reigned in Jerusalem one and thirty
years. And he did that which was right in the sight
of the Lord,…For in the eighth year of his reign,
while he was yet young, he began to seek after the
God of David his father: and in the twelfth year he
began to purge Judah and Jerusalem from the high
places, and the groves, and the carved images, and
the molten images. And they brake down the altars

of baalim in his presence; and the images, that were on high above them, he cut down; and the groves, and the carved images, and the molten images, he brake in pieces, and made dust of them, and strowed it upon the graves of them that had sacrificed unto them. And he burnt the bones of the priests upon their altars, and cleansed Judah and Jerusalem. And so did he in the cities of Manasseh, and Ephraim, and Simeon, even unto Naphtali, with their mattocks round about. And when he had broken down the altars and the groves, and had beaten the graven images into powder, and cut down all the idols throughout all the land of Israel, he returned to Jerusalem. Now in the eighteenth year of his reign, when he had purged the land, and the house, he sent Shaphan the son of Azaliah, and Maaseiah the governor of the city, and Joah the son of Joahaz the recorder, to repair the house of the Lord his God" (**2 Chronicles 34:1-8**).

You notice that it was only after Josiah had purged the land and his own house that he could face the house of the Lord to repair it. As long as idols are still present, you cannot afford to repair God's altar. God is a jealous God who shares His glory with no one. The worst sin Israel ever committed in the Old Testament was to worship other gods. When God forbade them from marrying foreign women, it was primarily because those women would potentially turn their hearts away from God to worship their idols.

King Josiah was young but brave; he resolved to put out all evil from the land of Judah and do what was right in the sight of God. The result of all he did was the outbreak of a mighty revival in the land. Dealing with idols is our sole responsibility. God will not come to help you take out idols from your life or Church. The Bible says,

"Draw nigh to God, and he will draw nigh to you. Cleanse your hands, ye sinners; and purify your hearts, ye double minded" (**James 4:8**).

Taking out idols is tantamount to cleansing our hands (remember, idols are the works of men's hands); deep repentance is a purification of our hearts. These are indispensable steps to restoration. Without these, any attempt to draw near to God would be fruitless lip service.

Once the glory of God departs from a Christian, it is likely that idols will fill that life. Remember that Satan works by substitution. He cannot lure a Christian out of intimacy with God and leave his or her life vacant. He usually fills such lives with his own stuff (the cares of this life, the deceitfulness of riches, religion, etc.).

As an example, let us consider the life and household of Jacob. Jacob, the supplanter, had many issues in his life. When he fled from his brother, Esau, he arrived in Luz, where he dreamt of the ladder and angels. Then he built an altar and named the place Bethel, vowing to return there and serve the Lord if the Lord would preserve him. We know his life thereafter with his uncle, Laban, and how he married Laban's two daughters and their maidservants. Upon his return from Laban, Jacob settled in Shechem. Then the Lord confronted him and told him to arise and go back to Bethel, the place of Divine encounter, the place where Jacob had vowed many years before to return to serve God. At the time of this confrontation, God wanted to restore Jacob. But first, Jacob had to return to Bethel and, of course, not without first purging his house.

"And God said unto Jacob, Arise, go up to Bethel, and dwell there: and make there an altar unto God

that appeared unto thee when thou fleddest from the face of Esau thy brother. Then Jacob said unto his household, and to all that were with him, Put away the strange God's that are among you and be clean, and change your garments: And let us arise, and go up to Bethel; and I will make there an altar unto God, who answered me in the day of my distress, and was with me in the way which I went. And they gave unto Jacob all their strange gods which were in their hands and all their earrings which were in their ears; and Jacob hid them under the oak which was by Shechem" (**Genesis 35:1-4**).

Why did the Lord not ask Jacob to just build an altar right where he was? Why did Jacob have to go back to Bethel? Notice that from Bethel, his life had experienced a decline, and so he had to return to *where* he had missed God. At Bethel, Jacob had vowed to return and serve the Lord, paying tithes of all things (**Genesis 28:20-22**). At this time, however, he had forgotten his vow and had erected an altar in a "strange land" called Shechem (**Genesis 33:18-20**). Even though he built an altar to the Lord at Shechem, the idols introduced into his house (possibly by Rachel — **Genesis 31:19, 34-35**) could not permit him to encounter God. This is why God rejected that altar and charged Jacob to return and build an altar in Bethel, knowing that Jacob could not return to Bethel without first dealing with the idols that had filled his house.

It is unimaginable that Jacob attempted serving the Lord when his house was filled with idols. We are told that Jacob erected an altar to the Lord in Shechem. How could he do this when his house was so polluted?

*"And Jacob came to Shalem, a city of Shechem,…
And he erected there an altar, and called it El-Elo-
he-Israel" (Genesis 33:18-20).*

The fact that God charged Jacob to return to Bethel
and build Him an altar there suggests that He did not
recognize and could not relate with the altar Jacob built
in Shechem. The reason was possibly two-fold: first, Jacob broke the vow he had made to return to Bethel; and
secondly, Jacob's life and household were not pure, as
we find that many idols were destroyed in his home before they could return to Bethel. What Jacob tried to do
in Shechem is exactly what some Christians do — they
sow among the thorns, caring little about first plowing
up their fallowed grounds through tearful repentance
with fasting.

With Jacob, it is important to note that the same Rachel whom he loved the most is the one who first introduced idols into his home. You should be careful with
what you love most. It can either become an idol or in-
troduce idols into your life. Whereas it is easy to allow
idols into one's heart, uprooting them is far from easy.
It amounts to peeling off the foreskin of our hearts (**Jeremiah 4:4**).

When Gideon was asked by the Lord to pull down
the altar his father had erected, it was going to be a big
risk (**Judges 6:25-27**). Read this passage and notice that
when parents lay ungodly foundations, their children
would be hindered and oppressed. The Angel of the
Lord visited the young man Gideon and God intended
to elevate and use Him as a deliverer for Israel. This was
Gideon's season of promotion, a time when the Lord
would catapult him from obscurity to prominence (raising him to the rank of Judge in Israel). But the idol Gideon's father worshipped stood in the way. God could do

nothing with Gideon as long as the altar of Baal was still in place. Although Gideon had managed to raise an altar to the Lord when he saw the angel (**Judges 6:24**), this could not be accepted as long as he had not dealt with the idol altar of his father. Thus, the Lord ordered Gideon to destroy the altar of Baal where his father continually worshipped. This was a necessary prerequisite for the restoration of Israel, which He wished to use Gideon to bring about.

You cannot worship the Lord in the same place where idols are. Idols have filled many Churches today and the Lord has quitted such Churches. Though people still try to worship God as Jacob did in Shechem, He is absent. Look keenly into your life and home. What is it that you must put out? An idol is not something that costs you anything. It is rather something very dear to your heart. Abraham loved Isaac so much and almost idolized him, so God demanded for Isaac. God said:

"...Take now thy son, thine only son Isaac, whom thou lovest...and offer him there for a burnt offering..." (**Genesis 22:2**).

If you want your life to count before God, the most precious things in your life must become a "burnt offering" for Him. Your idol could be a dress, a car, a house, a job, a pet, some artifact, jewelry, cosmetics, etc. Pray with all of your heart and God will not fail to show you what you must put out of your life as you seek to repair your altar and pursue the restoration of all that you've lost. It will be costly, painful, and difficult. You must be radical and you must not go into any negotiations with your flesh or the devil. It was not easy for young king Josiah to perform iconoclastic acts in Judah, pulling down all the high places. But God was with him as he walked and worked in obedience to God. The result was God's glory and revival in the land. If we truly desire full restoration, we must resolve, like King David, to set no wicked thing before us.

> "I will set no wicked thing before mine eyes: I hate the work of them that turn aside; it shall not cleave to me" (**Psalms 101:3**).

In conclusion, repairing your altar implies getting back to consistent prayer and Bible meditation, removing everything that offends. It implies getting back to true spiritual worship, having gotten rid of all forms of idols. The Apostle John said, "Little children, keep yourselves from idols. Amen" (**1 John 5:21**). This is because without this, we cannot maintain fellowship with God, causing our personal altars to crumble.

(3.) PROPHESYING TO THE DEAD BONES IN AND AROUND US

After repairing our altars, our last responsibility in restoration is to stand by our repaired altars and prophesy to the dead and dry bones of our lives, just as the Lord asked prophet Ezekiel to do to backslidden Israel. Most often, God works on earth through human vessels. Therefore, even in the matter of restoration, God seeks human vessels who can speak the word of faith over dead situations. Ezekiel, the prophet, was one such vessel in the time of Israeli captivity in Babylon. Ezekiel was qualified as a vessel of honor for God's use in bringing about restoration because although he was in captivity with the people of Israel, he was not a captive. He had a standing altar where he frequently encountered God. He had not joined Israel in their sins. He had remained faithful to God, and so his heavens were opened. It is such men that God seeks for use in revival and restoration. Those Christians with disintegrated altars may prophesy, but they are like clouds without water (**Jude 1:12**). The Lord has no regard for the words of such.

The reason why many people are prophesying to decayed situations today without results is because they are doing so by broken and unprepared altars. They have no ground on which they are standing in God's name. Elisha's servant, Gehazi, had no altar, and even when he was given the staff of his master to lay on a dead child in order to bring him back to life, he did so, but nothing happened (**2 Kings 4:29-31**). Elisha's staff was truly anointed, but the power therein was voided by a man without an altar. This seems to have been the only time Elisha witnessed a failure or disappointment in his ministry. Those without personal altars (that is, without a standing before God) command no authority before situations that require the move of God's power.

Let's get back to Prophet Ezekiel. He was God's Prophet in the time of Israel's captivity. The Lord sent him to proclaim His Word to those held captive. Periodically, the Lord would carry him in the Spirit to Jerusalem to show him the lamentable spiritual condition of Israel and the secret sins they committed, especially in the Temple. One of his encounters with the Lord, and the prophecy he was led to give, is instructive on the issue of pursuing restoration.

> "The hand of the Lord was upon me, and carried me out in the Spirit of the Lord, and set me down in the midst of the valley which was full of bones, And caused me to pass by them round about: and behold, there were very many in the open valley; and lo, they were very dry. And he said unto me, son of

man, can these bones live? And I answered, O Lord God, thou knowest. Again he said unto me, Prophesy upon these bones, and say unto them, O ye dry bones, hear the word of the Lord. Thus saith the Lord God unto these bones; Behold, I will cause breath to enter into you, and ye shall live: And I will lay sinews upon you, and will bring up flesh upon you, and cover you with skin, and put breath in you, and ye shall live; and ye shall know that I am the Lord. So I prophesied as I was commanded: and as I prophesied, there was a noise, and behold a shaking, and the bones came together, bone to his bone. And when I beheld, lo, the sinews and the flesh came up upon them, and the skin covered them above: but there was no breath in them. Then said He unto me, Prophesy unto the wind, prophesy, son of man, and say to the wind, Thus saith the Lord God; Come from the four winds, O breath, and breathe upon these slain, that they may live. So I prophesied as He commanded me, and the breath came into them, and they lived, and stood up upon their feet, an exceeding great army" **(Ezekiel 37:1-10)**.

There are four key issues we can draw from this passage that relate to restoration. <u>First</u>, no matter how dry and hopeless a situation is, there is always hope. God can do anything, any time, anyhow. Therefore, we should never lose hope. We are told that Abraham hoped against hope **(Romans 4:18)**. This was because he trusted in the Omnipotent God with whom nothing is impossible. Of course, he was not disappointed. Hope in the Lord does not disappoint us. Therefore, let us be hopeful in every situation. Above all, let us trust that the restoration of our lives, families, and ministries is a real possibility. It doesn't matter how low we have fallen. If we decide to arise and do the right things, God will do His part in restoring. The bones in the above passage looked so lifeless, hopeless, and scattered. It was quite a chaotic situation. However, God was still able to reverse the situation, as His servant, Ezekiel, did his part.

Second, only God can truly bring about restoration. Our responsibility in restoration is to prepare the way of the Lord (**Isaiah 40:3**), to cast up the highway, and to gather out the stones (**Isaiah 62:10**). Although the Lord would use human vessels, like Ezekiel, to pray and prophesy over spiritually dead conditions, it is Him who restores. This is why I am uncomfortable with those who claim the title of *"Revivalist."* The only true Revivalist is God Himself. When God asked Ezekiel *"Can these bones live?"* it was a test of his faith to see if Ezekiel trusted in himself to make them live. Ezekiel's response to God was quite witty. He said, *"O Lord God, thou knowest,"* which meant, *"Lord, if they can live, it depends on you."* In other words, Ezekiel understood that only God could determine the fate of those bones. If the bones would live, it would be the Lord's will. Ezekiel could have quickly or presumptuously said, "yes," as he was heavily anointed. Remember, the hand of the Lord was upon him mightily. When God releases His grace and anointing upon some people, they become presumptuous, thinking they could use the Holy Spirit at any time to do what they desire. Ezekiel knew better.

Third, God needs human vessels in restoration. We have analyzed the apostasy in the majority of Churches in our time. How will this situation be reversed? We can answer this question with another question: How did God reverse the oppressive situation in Israel each time they sinned and were judged in the era of the judges? God would always raise a judge whom He would anoint and use to deliver the land and bring about restoration.

God still works in the same way. For restoration to occur in today's Church, God seeks people whose hearts
are yearning for Him and who have not bowed the knee
to the idols of our time; He seeks men like Ezekiel. God
would have to raise anointed teachers of righteousness
to counteract the rampant false teachings crippling the
Church. We see in the above passage that although God
was burdened with the issue of restoring Israel, He
needed a person like Ezekiel to prophesy. Prophesying
over the dead is our duty. We do the prophesying and
God does the work. By prophecy here, I am not referring
to wishful utterances originating from selfish hearts. I
am referring to Holy Spirit-led utterances over negative
situations in our lives, families, Churches, or communities. Yes, if we are close to the Lord, those words of faith
would be given for us to speak as Ezekiel did speak. Notice that until Ezekiel began to speak, God did nothing.
We are told that confession is made unto salvation (**Romans 10:10**). This tells us how important it is to speak.
Believing in our hearts is not sufficient. Salvation comes
when the mouth gets involved in proclaiming the Holy
Ghost-breathed Word of faith.

Fourth, it will take the true Word of God to **mend**
and the Holy Spirit to **give life** to every dead situation. Realize that two things were necessary for life and
strength to return to the scattered bones: the words God
gave Ezekiel to speak and the East Wind. These two
things represent the pure Word of God and the Holy
Spirit. Without these two, restoration would be impossible. For restoration to occur in our Churches, the un-
adulterated Word of God must return to our pulpits.
Next, we must earnestly seek the Holy Spirit and have
Him move upon the Word. Only then can we hope for
conviction, deep repentance, and restoration. The pure
Word of God mends broken and scattered lives. How-

ever, it alone cannot give life. The letter kills and only the Holy Spirit quickens or gives life. Naturally, this leads us to the second major subsection of this chapter, which is God's part in procuring restoration.

THE DIVINE RESPONSIBILITY

When it comes to restoration, God takes the greater responsibility. He does the following:

(1.) HE POURS THE SPIRIT OF GRACE AND SUPPLICATIONS

"And I will pour upon the house of David, and upon the inhabitants of Jerusalem, the spirit of grace and of supplications: and they shall look upon me whom they have pierced, and they shall mourn for Him, as one mourneth for his only son, and shall be in bitterness for Him, as one that is in bitterness for his firstborn. In that day shall there be a great mourning in Jerusalem, as the mourning of Hadadrimmon in the valley of Megiddon. And the land shall mourn, every family apart; the family of the house of David apart, and their wives apart; the family of the house of Nathan apart, and their wives apart,...All families that remain, every family apart, and their wives apart" (**Zechariah 12:10-14**).

Although the above prophecy relates to Israel at the time of their final restoration, we can see that genuine repentance comes when God pours out the Spirit of grace and supplications. This is what brings deep conviction and contrition upon people's hearts. As mentioned previously, the nucleus of restoration or revival fire is usually a few people, or even a single person. God usually begins with a few people who can then build up the hedge and stand in the gap. As this small remnant cries out to God, He responds by pouring our His Spirit: the Spirit of grace and supplications. Without this, true repentance and restoration would be impossible. The Spirit of grace (to repent) and supplications (to beg God with tears) helps sinners and compromisers to see their true spiritual state, and consequently, burst out into tearful repentance. Some have gone too far into error, and their hearts have become so tough and fallowed that for those hearts to be softened and broken up again, this Spirit of grace and supplications must come upon them.

In general, when a person continues in an error for an extended period, the error looks like the truth, making it difficult to be convicted without God's help. This is the situation with most religious people. They have a form of godliness, but it is only an empty form because they deny the true power of a new life in Christ. Yet, because such religious folks have been deceived into believing they are on the right path and are saved, it is hard for them to get convicted without God's help. Therefore, as we seek restoration, we need to pray for the Lord to pour out the Spirit of Grace and supplications to convict sinners and bring about the kind of mourning described in **Joel 2**.

As mentioned regarding the Scriptures in **Zechariah 12:10-14**, God was speaking of what He would do to the Jews in the last days at the time of the restoration of all things. You notice in this passage that Israel would be unable to see or face their sins (that is, their rejection and crucifixion of the Messiah, and so on) until the Spirit of grace and supplications is poured upon them. Only then will they see Him, whom they pierced, and mourn in great bitterness.

The repentance will be thorough and not just a general cry. Every family shall mourn apart, wives apart, husbands apart, children apart, and so on. What does this mean? It implies that people will cry for their individual sins. They will call their sins by their names one by one and repent of them apart. The word **"apart"** is important in true repentance. You must face God as an individual, and thereafter, you can stand to intercede for others. Even if you are repenting in the midst of a crowd of 10,000 people in a conference, you still have to repent **apart**. Don't join the multitudes to say, "*Lord, if we have sinned against you, forgive us.*" You know your sins. Receive grace from God and call them by name in tears. Avoid using "if." True revival comes when people take responsibility over their wrongs and seek God decisively, calling their sins by name "apart." If you want true change, never shift the blame onto others. Arise and take responsibility.

(2.) HE JUDGES OUR ENEMIES

A time of restoration is a time when God arises like a travailing woman and contends with our enemies.

> "*The Lord shall go forth as a mighty man, He shall stir up jealousy like a man of war: He shall cry, yea, roar; He shall prevail against His enemies. I have long time holden my peace; I have been still, and refrained myself: now will I cry like a travailing woman; I will destroy and devour at once. I will make waste mountains and hills, and dry up all their herbs; and I will make the rivers islands, and I will dry up the pools. And I will bring the blind by a way that they*

knew not; I will lead them in paths that they have not known: I will make darkness light before them, and crooked things straight. These things will I do unto them, and not forsake them" (**Isaiah 42:13-16**).

God becomes jealous of His people when they repent. He causes double destruction in the enemy's camp, drying up every herb and stream. He turns all darkness into light and makes the crooked places straight.

"Shall the prey be taken from the mighty, or the lawful captive delivered? But thus saith the Lord, Even the captives of the mighty shall be taken away, and the prey of the terrible shall be delivered: for I will contend with him that contendeth with thee, and I will save thy children. And I will feed them that oppress thee with their own flesh; and they shall be drunken with their own blood, as with sweet wine: and all flesh shall know that I the Lord am thy Saviour and thy redeemer, the mighty One of Jacob" (**Isaiah 49:24-26**).

In a time of restoration, God takes us far from our enemies, feeding them with their flesh and blood. At such a time, He tells His people: "you shall be far from oppression and evil shall no longer come near your dwelling." He confronts our enemies Himself and delivers every captive that was **lawfully** in captivity. He gains honor over all our adversaries, just as He did over Pharaoh of Egypt. Note, however, that in our dispensation, we are not fighting flesh and blood as did the Israelis in the Old Testament. These enemies I am referring to are not primarily humans; they are spiritual forces and everything else that stands to oppose our lives.

Although in Christ, we have been given authority over spiritual forces, we lose this authority easily through disobedience to God (and His delegated authorities over us — such as parents and Church leaders). God gave authority to Adam over everything else He had created. But once Adam sinned, he lost that authority to Satan. The Church has lost her authority (that is, her Horse Gate) due to compromise or adulteration of God's Truth. A backslidden Christian or Church is a "prisoner of hope." Just as no prisoner can bail himself out of prison, neither can a backslider push back easily against Satan and his cohorts. Once a person is in prison, he or she needs external assistance to get out. For those in spiritual prisons, God promises to open their graves Himself and allow them to come out in a time of restoration.

> "...Thus saith the Lord God; Behold, O my people, I will open your graves, and cause you to come up out of your graves, and bring you into the land of Israel. And ye shall know that I am the Lord, when I have opened your graves, O my people, and brought you out of your graves" (**Ezekiel 37:12-13**).

Some Christians are in spiritual prisons or graves. It could be the prison of spiritual pride, prayerlessness, powerlessness, indiscipline, self-sufficiency, prodigality, addictions, an evil eye, an evil tongue, and so on. Many of those struggling with addictions have attempted many plausible solutions, but to no avail. I have met some of those people, and frankly, it's real bondage. Once a sinner or backslider repents sincerely, God forgives and intervenes to open prison doors and lead out the repentant soul. The repentant souls cannot suddenly lead their own selves out of prison. Let me illustrate with our Lord Jesus Christ. Our sins took Him to the grave, and while He was righteous, He still needed the assistance of the Holy Spirit to bring Him out of the grave (see **Romans 8:11**). Of course, when Jesus declared,"...*I have power to lay it (my life) down, and I have power to take it again...*" (**John10:18**), the power He referred to was that of the Holy Spirit. A time of restoration is a time of divine intervention. For example, when God does to us what He did to Peter, who was kept in prison awaiting slaughter (**Acts 12:3-11**). You see, Satan is never satisfied with just having a soul in captivity. Not only does he oppress that soul (like modern day terrorists do), but he also continues to nurse malicious plans towards that soul. Thus, we see that Satan stirred up Herod to arrest Peter and oppress him in prison. But this was not sufficient, as Herod planned on killing him eventually. As God foiled Herod's malicious plan against Peter (in response to the supplications of the Saints), so does He disappoint our enemies at a time of restoration. Not only does God intervene to foil their plots, He also destroys them, just as King Herod was (**Acts 12:20-24**). It is God's principle that whenever He delivers His people, He judges their enemies simultaneously. Recall, for example, His severe judgment upon the Egyptians. When God arises in a time of restoration and revival, He pleads with the enemies of His people (**Joel 3:1-2**). This is not a gentle pleading.

(3.) HE SENDS CORN, WINE, AND OIL IN ABUNDANCE

> "*Yea, the Lord will answer and say unto His people, Behold, I will send you corn, and wine, and oil, and ye shall be satisfied therewith: and I will no more make you a reproach among the heathen...Fear not, O land; be glad and rejoice: for the Lord will do great things....And the floors shall be full of wheat, and the fats shall overflow with wine and oil. And I will restore to you the years that the locust hath eaten,*

the cankerworm, and the caterpillar, and the palmer-worm, my great army which I sent among you. And ye shall eat in plenty, and be satisfied, and praise the name of the Lord your God that hath dealt wondrously with you: and my people shall never be ashamed" (**Joel 2:19, 21, 24-26**).

The Lord takes the responsibility of satisfying our needs in a time of restoration — needs of the body, the soul, and the spirit. Note the phrase in **verse 25**: *"And I will restore to you."* God said He would Himself restore. He didn't say, *"You will restore."* Again, restoration is not about us recovering things from the devil by ourselves, as some people teach. Many have tried in vain to recover by themselves, standing by broken altars and attempting to bind Satan. What we need to do is repair our altars and prepare the way of the Lord. We have then to stand by our repaired altars and prophesy as led by the Holy Spirit, and God would move as we so do. God promised to restore corn, wine, and oil. These symbolically summarize all human needs. **Corn** represents all we need as food, both physically and spiritually. **Wine** speaks of joy and represents all we need at the level of the soul and spirit to bring about peace, joy, and fulfillment. **Oil** speaks of *beauty* and represents all we need to make us attractive or charming, both physically and spiritually. Oil also speaks of anointing. God will not only restore these things, but will also provide them in abundance. Recall that famine is one of the curses God brings upon the rebellious (**Jeremiah 29:17-18**).

(4.) HE POURS OUT THE HOLY SPIRIT

"Be glad then, ye children of Zion, and rejoice in the Lord your God: for He hath given you the former rain

moderately, and He will cause to come down for you
the rain, the former rain, and the latter rain in the
first month. And it shall come to pass afterward, that
I will pour out my Spirit upon all flesh; and your
sons and your daughters shall prophesy, your old
men shall dream dreams, your young men shall see
visions" (**Joel 2:23, 28**).

God pours the Holy Spirit afresh in a time of restoration. In the first point of this subsection, we discussed
the Spirit of grace and supplications. This is the power
of the Holy Spirit bringing conviction and deep contrition upon people's hearts. The present point is meant to
emphasize more of what God's Holy Spirit does when
He comes at a time of restoration. Convicting of sin is
only the first step in His ministry in our lives and the
Church. The Holy Spirit is the one who carries out the
plans of the Godhead. Thus, we see Him at work during
creation; during the birth, ministration, and resurrection of our Lord Jesus Christ; and in the Early Church.
The Holy Spirit must, therefore, move mightily for restoration and revival to be possible.

In **Joel 2**, God promised an abundant outpour of His
Spirit following the fasting and repentance of His people. The former and latter rains do not normally fall in
the same month. Nevertheless, in a time of restoration,
both would fall in the same month (the first month).
This suggests a double blessing. Today, some Christians believe in a mighty end time revival that is yet to
come. Others contend that there can be no hope for revival given the ever-increasing degree of apostasy in the
end time Church. I would say restoration and revival
are possible if the Church would awaken, shake off the
dust of compromise, and prepare the way of the Lord.
If we arise and do the right things, God will respond to

us. God's promise is still true, that if His people called by His name shall humble themselves, pray, and turn from their evil ways, He would hear from heaven, forgive, and heal their land (**2 Chronicles 7:14**). This healing process is restoration.

When the Spirit comes, there are effects. People would prophesy, see visions, and dream dreams. This speaks volumes. There are many Churches today that believe in the baptism of the Holy Spirit with the evidence of speaking with new (unlearned) tongues and manifesting spiritual gifts. However, most of these manifestations have been corrupted due to spiritual decay. Many who were once enabled by the Holy Spirit to see true visions now see false visions motivated by their own lusts or demons that influence them. Lying prophets abound today, some of whom were once used by God. Time would fail me, enumerating some of the examples and clear false predictions they made. When God pours out His Holy Spirit afresh in a time of restoration, we will witness genuine Spirit-led manifestations with abiding results.

(5.) HE REPAIRS THE TABERNACLE OF DAVID

> *"In that day will I raise up the tabernacle of David that is fallen, and close up the breaches thereof; and I will raise up his ruins, and I will build it as in the days of old: That they may possess the remnant of Edom, and of all the heathen, which are called by my name, saith the Lord that doeth this"* (**Amos 9:11-12**).

In a time of restoration, God undertakes the repair of spiritual damages. The tabernacle of David speaks of bringing the presence of God into our lives and the

Church. The tabernacle of David was established when David prepared a tent for the Ark of God and brought it there (to the city of David). You can read about this in **1 Chronicles chapters 15 and 16**. You will realize that serious prayer, praise, and worship characterized the event. These are attributes of the tabernacle of David.

When God speaks of rebuilding the tabernacle of David, He is speaking of restoring true spiritual praise and worship to His Church, as well as the spirit of prayer and intercession. He is speaking of bringing His glory into our lives and the Church. David was indeed a man of intercession, praise, and worship. He was a psalmist and a skillful musician from his youth. He authored 73 of the Psalms in the Bible. Let's look at a few of David's confessions in the Psalms.

"My voice shalt thou hear in the morning, O Lord; in the morning will I direct my prayer unto thee, and look up" (**Psalms 5:3**).

David was determined to pray every morning, just like the Lord Jesus Christ. He covenanted with God to have his voice heard in heaven every morning. This speaks to the level of personal discipline that David had regarding his walk with the Lord. He was a man of prayer.

"Give unto the Lord the glory due unto His name; worship the Lord in the beauty of holiness" (**Psalms 29:2**).

David was also a man who worshipped God in the beauty of holiness and called on others to join him do so. A sinner or hypocrite cannot worship God in the beauty of holiness. Today, there are many people lifting up defiled hands to the Father in the name of spiritual worship. Worship is sacred, and there is nothing as offensive to God as a profane or defiled man or an idolater coming before Him in worship. This is why He told sinful Israelites:

> "...The incense you bring me is a stench in my nostrils. Your holy celebrations...and your special days for fasting (even your most pious meetings) all are frauds! I want nothing more to do with them all; I can't stand the sight of them" (**Isaiah 1:11-14, L.B.**).

This is God's attitude toward any person coming before Him who lives a life of sin and who ignores his or her sin. In a time of restoration when God rebuilds the Tabernacle of David, genuine worship and praise return to the Church as the people's lives are purified. God still seeks faithful worshippers who would worship Him in spirit and in truth.

> "But the hour cometh and now is, when the true worshippers shall worship the Father in spirit and in truth: for the Father seeketh such to worship Him. God is a Spirit: and they that worship Him **must** worship Him in spirit and in truth" (**John 4:23-24**).

This is the prescribed acceptable form of worship that God promises to restore to the Church. Today, we have people drawing near to God with their lips, but with their hearts, they are far away in the world. Moreover, much of today's Gospel music has been corrupted. Some of today's Gospel songs enhance self rather than exalt the Lord. Just take a look at Church hymns, most of which were written in the 1700s, 1800s and early 1900s. When one sings those hymns, one finds an indelible passion toward the Lord (and His glory) in the hearts of the authors of those songs. Such passion for godliness and the exaltation of the Lord is largely absent in modern Gospel music. Restoring the Tabernacle of David also entails removing the corruption from the music of the Church.

Lastly, David confesses:

"But I will hope continually, and will yet praise thee more and more" (**Psalms 71:14**).

David was a man of great faith. He knew the Lord was his Shepherd. Thus, he praised the Lord daily, regardless of his condition. No adverse condition could stop him from praising the Lord. The character traits of David are attributes of the tabernacle of David, the man after God's heart. This passion is what God plans to restore to the Church in a time of revival.

CHAPTER SEVEN

THE EFFECTS OF RESTORATION

This final chapter overlaps somewhat with some of the issues discussed in the previous chapter regarding the "Divine Responsibility" in restoration. The current chapter sheds further light on this. Understanding some of the glories of restoration will motivate us to pursue restoration in a sustainable way until we witness it. Some Bible chapters, including **Isaiah 32:14-20, Isaiah 49:8-26, Isaiah 60-62 and Amos 9:11-15**, describe the effects and results of restoration. You will do well to study these passages in your own time. Although these Bible passages talk of the restoration of Israel, we must understand that Israel in the Old Testament is a picture of the Church in the New Testament. We will now discuss some of the blessings that come with biblical restoration.

(1.) GOD'S ABIDING GLORY DRAWING MANY TO SALVATION — GROWTH

"...but the Lord shall arise upon thee, and His glory shall be seen upon thee. And the gentiles shall come to thy light, and kings to the brightness of thy rising.... Then thou shalt see, and flow together, and thine heart shall fear, and be enlarged; because the abundance of

the sea shall be converted unto thee, the forces of the
gentiles shall come unto thee" (**Isaiah 60:2-5**).

It takes but the glory of God shining through the
Church to draw the world to Christ. When we fall short
of this glory, no amount of effort can draw the people.
A time of restoration is a time when God's glory re-
turns with the result of many turning to righteousness.
Restoration leads to Church expansion and missionary
work. There will be rapid multiplication, such that one
becomes 1,000 and a small one becomes a strong nation
(**Isaiah 60:22**). In the previous chapter, we noted that
God responds to our cries for restoration by pouring out
His Spirit afresh. The result of this outpouring is that
His glory is revealed and the abundance of the sea (the
world) is converted. Take a look at the outpouring of
the Holy Spirit on the day of Pentecost (**Acts 2**) and the
results that ensued. Whereas many pastors are laboring and finding new strategies to grow their Churches,
when the Spirit of God is poured, souls will be drawn
to the Churches with little effort or strategic planning.

(2.) HONOR OF GOD'S PEOPLE

"The sons also of them that afflicted thee shall come
bending unto thee; and all they that despised thee
shall bow themselves down at the soles of thy feet; and
they shall call thee, The city of the Lord, the Zion of
the Holy One of Israel. Whereas thou hast been for-
saken and hated, so that no man went through thee,
I will make thee an eternal excellency, a joy of many
generations" (**Isaiah 60:14-15**).

God's glory upon our lives is our honor. You will
find this glory upon Abraham. He didn't have many

people with him. However, the heathen nations around him always feared him and regarded him as a mighty prince. This was the result of God's glory upon his life and household. When God's glory abides over our lives and Churches, there will be a reputation and our enemies will be in fear. When the Canaanite kings around the Jordan River heard that Israel had crossed the river, their hearts melted and they lost courage (**Joshua 5:1**). This was the result of God's glory upon His people. This glory brought fear upon their enemies.

When God's people backslide or get into apostasy, God's glory is lost and they become oppressed. Jeremiah asked three important questions about backslidden Israel:

"Is Israel a servant? is he a homeborn slave? why is he spoiled?" (**Jeremiah 2:14**).

Due to Israel's backsliding, she had become a servant, a home born slave, completely robbed and left naked. There is much correlation between this and what the Church has lost in our time, as was discussed previously. During a time of restoration, God brings back His glory and His people are honored. The result is that those who mocked the Church or God's people would no longer do so. Many people are eager to obtain honor and recognition from men.

Unfortunately, they do not know how to. Some of them are fighting to obtain multiple titles (and sometimes doing so through unscrupulous means) as a means of becoming dignified. Contrarily, we see that most of Christ's apostles were ordinary men with no education. However, the Lord honored them by allowing His great grace to rest upon them. There is an honor that only comes from God (**John 5:44**). We must each seek this honor. It comes automatically when God restores our lives.

During restoration, the previously despised Christian becomes a force to be reckoned with; the Church that few visited previously becomes a source of joy for many generations. For each of us, this means that God will not only use us to meet immediate needs, but will also use us to do things that go into historical records or leave indelible marks for years. Our shame will be transformed into the true aroma of Christ and we will be given a new name.

> "...and thou shall be called by a new name, which the mouth of the Lord shall name. Thou shall also be a crown of glory in the hand of the Lord, and a royal diadem in the hand of thy God. Thou shalt no more be termed Forsaken; neither shall thy land any more be termed Desolate: but thou shalt be called Hephzibah, and thy land Beulah: for the Lord delighteth in thee, and thy land shall be married" (**Isaiah 62:2-4**).

The name **Hephzibah** means: "*My delight is in her,*" while the name **Beulah** means: "*She is married.*" What name do you have presently? Do you have a particular problem with what people call you? The Bible says Jesus was in the house of "*Simon the leper*" when Mary came to anoint Him (**Matthew 26:6-7**). What troubles me is the fact that Jesus was in this leper's house and yet his name remained "the leper." He had been permanently labelled with his problem. Yes, Jesus can be somewhere, and yet, many do not benefit. He got to Nazareth and couldn't do any miracles apart from heal a few sick folks due to the people's lack of belief (**Mark 6:1-4**).

When we resolve to pursue restoration, God responds by giving us a new name. For example, from *"disgrace, shame, or forsaken"* to *"honor or favor."* A time of restoration is also called the time of the Lord's favor or the acceptable year of the Lord, which is when He glorifies His people (**Isaiah 49:8**). It is a time when God's delight is in His people and His marriage vow with them is renewed.

(3.) RESTFULNESS

> *"Violence shall no more be heard in thy land, wasting nor destruction within thy borders; but thou shalt call thy walls Salvation, and thy gates Praise"* (**Isaiah 60:18**). *"And my people shall dwell in a peaceable habitation, and in sure dwellings, and in quiet resting places"* (**Isaiah 32:18**).

The effect of backsliding is the destruction of our walls of protection, and consequently, the absence of peace. When the hedge is broken, serpents bite us. During restoration, the Lord deals with all our foes (as we saw in the previous chapter) and grants us all rest. This state of restfulness implies the absence of internal and external battles. The result is that we would dwell in peaceful habitations. I know you may be asking, *"Does Ephesians 6:12-13 cease to exist?"* Although the devil and his demons are still there, they can do little to oppose or cause any sort of harm to God's people in a time of restoration. At a time of restoration, God makes His people like the Prophet Jeremiah, of whom He testified:

> *"And I will make thee unto this people a fenced brazen wall: and they shall fight against thee, but they shall not prevail against thee: for I am with thee to save thee and to deliver thee, saith the Lord. And I will deliver thee out of the hand of the wicked, and*

I will redeem thee out of the hand of the terrible"
(**Jeremiah 15:20-21**).

This is what God does in a time of restoration. He
makes His people a fortified city to protect them against
enemy aggression. King David walked with God, and
because of this, Israel was restored and established in
his reign. After him, King Solomon enjoyed an era of
peacefulness in Israel because the Lord had fortified the
nation and fenced it with spiritual brazen walls, so to
speak. When God restores us, we become like fortified
cities that cannot be easily broken by the enemy. The
Lord undertakes to defend His people fully and to keep
them at rest, preparing a table for them in the very presence of their enemies. Today, it is not uncommon to find
people in Churches who are spiritually destitute and
oppressed by Satan and his elements. In a time of restoration, God dislodges the enemy and brings His people
to a large place. He leads the blind by a way they knew
not.

(4.) Sorrow Banished, with the Full Return of Joy and Gladness

*"Thy sun shall no more go down; neither shall thy
moon withdraw itself: for the Lord shall be thine everlasting light, and the days of thy mourning shall
be ended"* (**Isaiah 60:20**). *"When the Lord turned
again the captivity of Zion, we were like them that
dream. Then was our mouth filled with laughter, and
our tongue with singing: then said they among the
heathen, The Lord hath done great things for them.
The Lord hath done great things for us; whereof we
are glad"* (**Psalms 126:1-3**).

Restoration is the turning again of our captivity, and when this happens, we cannot help but laugh. In today's Church, some are sorrowful, perhaps due to a barren situation, the absence of marriage, an affliction of their bodies, and so on. In many instances, the Daughter of Zion has been robbed of her joy. Some Christians are managing to obey the command to "rejoice always," while their hearts (in reality) are sorrowful or bleeding. When God heals and delivers in a time of restoration, joy and genuine laughter return to Zion. Inner healing would translate to God's previously oppressed people receiving beauty for ashes, the oil of joy for mourning, and the garment of praise for the spirit of heaviness (**Isaiah 61:3**).

(5.) ABIDING RIGHTEOUSNESS

"Then judgment shall dwell in the wilderness, and righteousness remain in the fruitful field. And the work of righteousness shall be peace; and the effect of righteousness quietness and assurance forever" (**Isaiah 32:16-17**). *"Thy people also shall be all righteous: they shall inherit the land for ever, the branch of my planting, the work of my hands, that I may be glorified"* (**Isaiah 60:21**).

Hypocrisy disappears during restoration. God purges His Church from all filth and puts His spirit in the people, according to **Ezekiel 36:26-27**, causing them to walk in total obedience. The Church ceases to be a place for "mixed multitude." The fear of the Lord comes upon the Church in a time of restoration. Such a fear came upon the early Church after Ananias and Sapphira were slain (**Acts 5:1-11**). Even the life that was initially a spiritual wilderness becomes filled with justice and truth.

God's people are transformed in a time of restoration into a people of integrity with which one could do business freely and without fear of being robbed or cheated.

(6.) SACRIFICIAL SERVICE TO THE LORD

"And strangers shall stand and feed your flocks, and the sons of the alien shall be your plowmen and your vinedressers. But ye shall be named the Priests of the Lord: men shall call you the Ministers of our God: ye shall eat the riches of the gentiles, and in their glory shall you boast yourselves" (**Isaiah 61:5-6**).

In our backsliding, we rise up early every day and labor after worldly things, eating the bread of sorrows (**Psalms 127:2**). But during restoration, God's people become *"the Priests of the Lord; the ministers of our God."* This means that restoration redirects the attention of God's people away from worldly pursuits. Restoration restores our passion for service in God's Kingdom and helps us awake to that responsibility. God's people are willing in the day of His power, the day of restoration (**Psalms 110:3**). We will labor for the Lord without murmuring, testifying of His wondrous love and care, while gathering jewels for their crowns above. Before restoration, a Church of 2,000 members may only have 50 laborers (or less) who are staff members on payroll. But when God brings about restoration, many people in the Church begin to take initiative and engage in voluntary services for God's glory.

Without restoration, a pastor may preach and teach about serving God and the rewards awaiting servants, but few in his Church may actually commit to serving the Lord in a measurable way. Most people will not put the world behind unless the "day of God's power"

COST AND EFFECTS OF RESTORATION 165

comes. This day is the day when God chooses to release His Spirit afresh and touch men. **Isaiah 61:5-6** tells us that as we serve the Lord, others will serve us: feeding our flocks and being our ploughmen and wine dressers.

When we offer ourselves wholly to God and His purposes, He takes care of us, raising people to serve us. This is awesome! I have many testimonies of people serving me. Part of this service was them providing for my needs. I recall when I just came to the Lord and my family held a meeting to terminate my education because I became born again. The money that was set aside for transporting my furniture, books, and other possessions from my school back to our family home ended up being used to pay my tuition that year. God turned the situation completely around, and so what was meant for evil, ended up serving me.

(7.) THE DOUBLE BLESSING

The word "**double**" is characteristic of restoration. In His graciousness, God usually desires to make the restored much more glorious than what was lost. God did promise to make the latter house (what is restored) much more glorious than the former (what was lost) (**Haggai 2:9**).

> "Comfort, oh, comfort my people, says your God. Speak tenderly to Jerusalem and tell her that her sad days are gone. Her sins are pardoned, and the Lord will give her twice as many blessings as He gave her punishments before" (**Isaiah 40:1, L.B.**). "For your shame you shall have double; and for confusion they shall rejoice in their portion: therefore in their land they shall possess the double: everlasting joy shall be unto them" (**Isaiah 61:7**). "Turn ye to the strong-

hold, ye prisoners of hope: even today do I declare that
I will render double unto thee" (**Zechariah 9:12**).

All these scriptures speak of God's mind and promises for restoration. God's desire is not just to bring back
what we lost, but also to bring back much more. A time
of restoration is a time of great prosperity or abundance
(both spiritually and materially). It is a time when God
brings back double of everything that was stolen from
His people.

I am mindful of all that's out there; that is, the prosperity Gospel with many deceivers making merchan-
dise of simple-minded Christians. What I am writing
here is in no way related to that. While we must never
set our minds on earthly possessions, we need to realize
that when God restores His people, they prosper in all
aspects. In a time of captivity, the people toil and reap
little from their labor; they obtain money only to place
it in pockets with holes. When God restores us, the situation is different. At a time of restoration, we would
plant vineyards and eat their fruit; fruitless labors or en-
deavors would vanish.

A time of restoration is a time of overflow.

"And the floors shall be full of wheat, and the fats
shall overflow with wine and oil" (**Joel 2:24**).

Remember that **wine** speaks of joy and **oil** speaks of
beauty and the anointing. When God restores us, these
virtues will overflow in our lives and bless those around
us. The Scripture will be fulfilled where Jesus spoke of
rivers of living water flowing out of our bellies.

It is the time of double harvest.

"Behold, the days come, saith the Lord, that the plow-man shall overtake the reaper, and the treader of grapes him that soweth seed; and the mountains shall drop sweet wine, and all the hills shall melt. And I will bring again the captivity of my people of Israel, and they shall build the waste cities, and inhabit them; and they shall plant vineyards, and drink the wine thereof; they shall also make gardens, and eat the fruit of them" (**Amos 9:13-14**).

As mentioned above, our labors will yield tangible fruits in a time of restoration. We won't labor in vain or plant and have others harvest. You see, planting only to have others harvest is a curse. In the Mosaic Law, the Lord forbade certain people from going to war. These included those who recently got married, those who built a new house but had not dedicated it, those who were engaged but yet to be married, and those who had planted vineyards but had not eaten the fruits of their labor (**Deuteronomy 20:5-7; 24:5**).

This shows us how God does not like to see His people labor without enjoying the fruits of their labor. The Scriptures say, *"The husbandman that laboureth must be first partaker of the fruits"* (**2 Timothy 2:6**). In a time of backsliding, however, God's people travail but give birth to wind; they wrought no righteousness, no deliverance, and little or no prosperity (**Isaiah 26:18**).

When God restores, however, the plowmen (among the heathen) overtake the reapers (in God's Kingdom). What does this mean? We understand this by recalling God's promise to send the former and latter rains in the same first month (see **Joel 2:23**). How possible is this? It is impossible with men, but not with God; with God, all things are possible. When God speaks of the plowman overtaking the reaper in **Amos 9**, He means that He would bless His people in such a way that they would sow and harvest so much. They would continue to harvest until the next planting season. When the heathen are plowing their ground for the next season of planting, God's people will still be harvesting. In this way, the plowmen among the heathen will overtake the reapers among God's people. This is what God means by the plowman overtaking the reaper. It is because the reaper will be so blessed that he reaps into the next season of planting.

It is a time of Divine replacements.

"For brass I will bring gold, and for iron I will bring silver, and for wood brass, and for stones iron: I will also make thy officers peace, and thine exactors righteousness" (**Isaiah 60:17**).

This Scripture, once more, shows God's intent to restore us to a more glorious state. If you lose brass, you will get back gold; and if you lose iron, you will receive silver in return, and so on. Of course, you know that gold is better than brass and silver is better than iron. A time of restoration is a time when God gives beauty for ashes, the oil of joy for mourning, and the garment of praise for the spirit of heaviness, to the extent that His people become His very planting, building up ruined places, and so on (**Isaiah 61:1-9**).

All of this is not intended by God to boast our ego. It is intended for His glory. He exalts His people in a time of restoration for His own glory. He exalted Job to be the greatest man in the East (**Job 1:1-3**). He exalted Abraham to be a mighty prince. He did all of these for His glory, not to boast the ego of these people. God, likewise, exalts His people in a time of restoration in order to bring glory to His name.

(8.) TRUE WORSHIP

"And ye shall eat in plenty, and be satisfied, and Praise the name of the Lord your God that hath dealt wondrously with you: and my people shall never be ashamed" (**Joel 2:26**).

It takes real maturity for a man in pain or serious need to continue praising the Lord in his unchanged condition. True worship is scarce in the Church today, partly because many are hurting spiritually, emotionally, or physically. With these, only the spiritually mature still rejoice and worship God with outbursts of joy. Most others are simply religious, drawing near with lips, and hence, worshiping in vain.

In a time of restoration, however, every yoke gets broken, and God's people are liberated in all areas of their lives. This in no way suggests that all problems cease. To be liberated is not equivalent to stating that all problems have been vanquished. Of course, a time of great revival can also be a time of great persecution, as we find with the early disciples in the Acts of the Apostles. However, we also find that those early disciples were continually filled with joy. This is a clear sign that they were fully liberated from all bondage and lived only for God's glory. Therefore, external problems, such as persecution, had no impact on their souls and spirits. The result was that they worshipped God, often in Spirit and in Truth.

When God satisfies our needs in a time of restoration, the result is true and spontaneous worship. As stated above, it is hard to do so while in captivity. For example, the Israelites were unable to worship the Lord in their captivity.

*"By the rivers of Babylon, there we sat down, yea, we wept, when we remembered Zion. We hanged our harps upon the willows in the midst thereof. For there they that carried us away captive required of us a song; and they that wasted us required of us mirth, saying, Sing us one of the songs of Zion. **How shall we sing the Lord's song in a strange land?"*** **(Psalms 137:1-4)**.

It is not possible to sing the Lord's song of worship in a strange land or in a backslidden state. After restoration, your joy returns and you have the liberty again to worship God in the beauty of holiness.

The above eight points are but a few out of the many glories of restoration. May these serve as motivation for you to pursue the full restoration of your own life, family, or Church.

CONCLUSION

This book discussed critical questions about the issue of the restoration of our individual lives and Churches to the state that God desires. God's plan is for us to grow into "a perfect man," to the measure of the statue of the fullness of Christ. This is why He gave spiritual gifts to His Church (see **Ephesians 4:11-13**).

Sadly, much of what we read in the Bible is only theoretical to the Church during this time. Much has been lost and the Church has been largely corrupted. The Church today looks much like a money-making enterprise (disguised as a non-profit organization) for the enrichment of the clergy. Most of our shepherds are fattening themselves instead of God's flock. Many different tares have been sown at different points in history while men slept. The demarcation between the Church and the world continues to fade away, as we draw near to the return of our Lord.

Although our Lord Jesus Christ foreknew this and cried, "*...when the Son of man cometh, shall he find faith on the earth?*" (**Luke 18:8**), it is my belief that restoration is still possible for those who care. God never despises a broken and contrite spirit. God cannot perpetually ignore people who have resolved to part with all iniquity and agonize before Him day and night for the restoration of their lives, families, Churches, and communities.

This book has shown in detail what the Church has lost, as well as why it was lost, where it was lost, and how to pursue restoration. Without knowing what we lost, we won't know what to pursue. Without knowing

why we lost it, we could lose it again, even if we recover it. Without knowing where we lost it, we could
underestimate recovery efforts or come up shy of full
restoration.

For example, Elisha set out to pray for the resurrection of a dead child. After his first round of intense
prayers, even stretching himself over the corpse, the
child became warm, but was still dead. Elisha could
have ended his prayers at that point. If he did, the child
would get cold again and would eventually be buried.
When the awareness of the need for restoration dawns
on some Christians, they pray only to the stage of getting their "dead child" (the things they lost) warm. But
those who want full restoration must press beyond this
point — and Elisha knew this. He paced back and forth
in the room and engaged in the second round of intense
prayer, again stretching himself on the dead child. Even
after this second phase, the child was still dead. The
child sneezed once, but there was no life. As Elisha persisted in prayer, the child sneezed a second time, then
a third time, up to a seventh time. At the seventh time,
full life returned to the child. He opened his eyes and sat
up. The full account of this miracle is given below:

> "And when the child was grown, it fell on a day, that
> he went out to his father to the reapers. And he said
> unto his father, My head, my head. And he said to a
> lad, Carry him to his mother. And when he had taken
> him, and brought him to his mother, he sat on her
> knees till noon, and then died. And she went up, and
> laid him on the bed of the man of God, and shut the
> door upon him, and went out. And she called unto her
> husband, and said, Send me, I pray thee, one of the
> young men, and one of the asses, that I may run to the
> man of God, and come again. And he said, Wherefore

wilt thou go to him today? it is neither new moon, nor sabbath. And she said, It shall be well. Then she saddled an ass, and said to her servant, Drive, and go forward; slack not thy riding for me, except I bid thee. So she went and came unto the man of God to mount Carmel. And it came to pass, when the man of God saw her afar off, that he said to Gehazi his servant, Behold, yonder is that Shunammite: Run now, I pray thee, to meet her, and say unto her, Is it well with thee? is it well with thy husband? is it well with the child? And she answered, It is well: And when she came to the man of God to the hill, she caught him by the feet: but Gehazi came near to thrust her away. And the man of God said, Let her alone; for her soul is vexed within her: and the Lord hath hid it from me, and hath not told me. Then she said, Did I desire a son of my lord? did I not say, Do not deceive me? Then he said to Gehazi, Gird up thy loins, and take my staff in thine hand, and go thy way: if thou meet any man, salute him not; and if any salute thee, answer him not again: and lay my staff upon the face of the child. And the mother of the child said, As the Lord liveth, and as thy soul liveth, I will not leave thee. And he arose, and followed her. And Gehazi passed on before them, and laid the staff upon the face of the child; but there was neither voice, nor hearing. Wherefore he went again to meet him, and told him, saying, The child is not awaked. And when Elisha was come into the house, behold, the child was dead, and laid upon his bed. He went in therefore, and shut the door upon them twain, and prayed unto the Lord. And he went up, and lay upon the child, and put his mouth upon his mouth, and his eyes upon his eyes, and his hands upon his hands: and stretched himself upon the child; and the flesh of the child waxed warm. Then he returned, and

walked in the house to and fro; and went up, and
stretched himself upon him: and the child sneezed
seven times, and the child opened his eyes. And he
called Gehazi, and said, Call this Shunammite. So he
called her. And when she was come in unto him, he
said, Take up thy son. Then she went in, and fell at his
feet, and bowed herself to the ground, and took up her
son, and went out" (**2 Kings 4:18-37**).

As we conclude this book, our prayer is that you will act like the Shunammite woman in the above passage. When her only child died, she knew where to go for help. Did you notice that she did not even tell her husband about the death of their son? When she sent servants to him in the fields, it was only to request one of the servants and an ass. When her husband wondered why should would visit the Prophet on an odd day, she still didn't tell him their son had passed away. She knew that her sweet husband could not help her in that situation. Many of us cry to the wrong people; we tell our problems to those who cannot help us. Learn to take your issues to the Lord. Elisha, in the above passage, is a picture of our Lord, who Himself said: "...*I am the resurrection, and the life...*" (**John 11:25**).

The Shunammite hurried to meet Elisha for the resurrection of her child. If the Holy Spirit has touched your heart and convinced you of your need of restoration through this book, do not procrastinate your response. You need to make haste in returning to the Lord. Do not stop to be entertained by "Gehazi." Although Gehazi was Elisha's servant, the Shunammite also knew he couldn't help her. So when Gehazi asked her, "*Is it well with thee? is it well with thy husband? Is it well with the child?*", her quiet response to him was, "*It is well.*" Do not waste time with mere mortals; they can't help you secure restoration. The Shunammite knew this. She pressed on until she found Elisha and caught him by the feet, as if to say, "you are not going from here unless you solve my problem." Her taking hold of Elisha's feet was a prostration, a sign of deep reverence for Elisha and of brokenness and supplication. Although Gehazi felt she disrespected his master and came to thrust her away, Elisha stopped him, acknowledging she was in agony of soul. It is our prayer that each of us will be in agony of soul after reading this book, and consequently, press on, seeking restoration.

When Elisha sent his staff with his servant, Gehazi, to be laid on the dead child, the Shunammite persisted until Elisha arose to go with her. After Elisha charged Gehazi to go with her, she refused saying, "*As the Lord liveth, and as thy soul liveth, I will not leave thee.*" She acted much like Moses, who refused to go with an Angel of the Lord, but urged God to go with him and with Israel. We see that if this woman was not persistent and determined to see her dead child resurrected, that child would have been buried. Seeking restoration, especially in the perilous times in which we live, is a costly venture, requiring an inner resolve to not quit. May the Lord bless your spirit and use this book to kindle such a resolve in you, as you arise to seek restoration, and may God bring you (and your family or ministry) to full restoration. Amen.

For more copies or speaking engagements:

Author Contact:

Patrick Tamukong, Ph.D.
E-mail: ptamukong@yahoo.com

IEM PRESS

Inspire, Equip, & Motivate

To order additional copies of this book call:
214-908-3963
or visit our website at
www.iempublishing.com

If you enjoyed this quality custom-published book,
drop by our website for more books and information.

"Inspiring, Equipping and Motivating Publishing"

www.ingramcontent.com/pod-product-compliance
Lightning Source LLC
LaVergne TN
LVHW051053080426
835508LV00019B/1844